GLENN

GLENN

David Young

COACH HOUSE PRESS   TORONTO

This play is fully protected under the copyright laws of Canada and all other countries of the Copyright Union and is subject to royalty. Changes to the script are expressly forbidden without the written consent of the author. Rights to produce, film, record in whole or in part, in any medium or in any language, by any group, *amateur or professional*, are retained by the author. Interested persons are requested to apply for permission and terms to:

Coach House Press, 401 (rear) Huron Street,
Toronto, Ontario, Canada M5S 2G5.

Author's acknowledgments: Thanks to Richard Rose, Paul Ledoux and Don Kugler who helped me find and focus this play. The Toronto Arts Council, the Canada Council and the Ontario Arts Council provided vital support during the early stages of development; special thanks also to George D. Butterfield and Jill Fraser who came through when the chips were down. This project was developed with the permission of the Estate of Glenn Gould and Glenn Gould Limited.

Published with the assistance of the Canada Council, the Ontario Arts Council and the Ontario Ministry of Culture and Communications.

Canadian Cataloguing in Publication Data
Young, David, 1946-
   Glenn

A play.
ISBN 0-88910-429-8

1. Gould, Glenn, 1932-1982 - Drama.   I. Title.

PS8597.085G5 1992   C812'.54   C92-095116-3
PR9199.3.Y68G5 1992

CONTENTS

THE INTERVAL

ACT II

FOREWORD

In 1977, when my book *Glenn Gould, Music and Mind* was in production at Van Nostrand Reinhold in Toronto, I accepted an invitation to give a lecture to a group of information theorists and cognitive psychologists at the University of Toronto. I decided to call my lecture 'Many voices: the polyphony of Glenn Gould.' When I submitted my title for the advance notice of the lecture, the convener of the group glanced at it and snorted: 'That's jargon! Nobody will know what that's about!' As an alternative he suggested 'Parallel processing of multiple inputs: the case of Glenn Gould.' I was so amused by his insistence that 'polyphony' is jargon, while 'parallel processing etc.' is not, that I agreed to this. As it turned out, there was a good attendance at my lecture, whatever that proves.

I needed no probe of his brain, no scope, scan or gram, to demonstrate that Glenn Gould had a remarkable capacity for sorting and controlling a multiplicity of concurrent mental processes. For my evidence I needed only to point to his works, particularly his recordings of many-voiced (i.e. 'polyphonic') compositions for keyboard, e.g. a fugue by Bach or a fantasia by Gibbons. In these recordings he gave each 'voice' in the music a distinctive character, while never permitting any of them to assert themselves to the detriment of the ensemble or of the structure. It was almost unanimously agreed that no other keyboard player of his time surpassed Gould in this respect.

For most of his working life, Glenn Gould's habitat was the sound studio: darkness, mysterious apparatus, a few harsh utility lights, blinking monitors. Such is the setting of the play *Glenn*. The treatment of characters in the play is equally felicitous. Gould was a complex person, indeed, he was a blithely multiple person, as witness those of his writings in which he featured himself in various roles. *Glenn* puts Gould before us as not one but four characters: Prodigy, Performer, Perfectionist, Puritan. These four are the dramatis personae, although occasionally one or the other of them doubles nimbly as someone else, e.g. Theodore Slutz, Dr. Wolfgang von Krankmeister, even Herbert von Karajan. There are only four characters, but there are many voices in the play, just as there were in its namesake.

Like most of Gould's recordings and writings, the play is busy, with its interlocking themes and multiple levels, each distinct but none dominant, and with its disregard for chronology. Time is stretched, squeezed, interrupted, reversed, lapped and bent, all in ways familiar to musicians. In this respect the play resembles Gould's so-called 'contrapuntal radio documentaries,' audiotape collages the making of which was for ten years his main artistic endeavour, ending in 1979 with his documentary on Richard Strauss. These works, which Gould regarded as musical compositions, have in recent years had less attention than they deserve, for which reason I welcome the release by CBC Records of Gould's documentaries 'The Idea of North,' 'The Latecomers' and 'Quiet in the Land' in a boxed set entitled *The Solitude Trilogy*.

I predict that David Young's *Glenn*, like Gould's documentaries, will find little favour with people who see nothing wrong with the idea of naming a concert hall or a piano competition after Glenn Gould. Such people have missed the point of Gould's entire achievement.

Glenn is neither a delightful and relaxing entertainment nor, in its published form, an 'easy read.' In my opinion, it is something much better: a faithful and worthy evocation of its subject.

Geoffrey Payzant
Toronto, August 1992

Art, on its loftiest mission, is hardly human at all.

—Glenn Gould

GLENN

Production History

Glenn was first produced by the Necessary Angel Theatre
Company at the duMaurier Theatre Centre in Toronto
as part of the Glenn Gould Festival, in September 1992.

Directed by Richard Rose
Dramaturgy by Paul Ledoux and Don Kugler
Musical Direction by Don Horsburgh
Set and Lighting Design by Graeme S. Thomson
Costume Design by Charlotte Dean
Choreography by Susan McKenzie
Sound Design by Richard Mendonca
Stage Managed by Debra McKay
assisted by Cara Millson

Cast
THE PRODIGY, Duncan Ollerenshaw
THE PERFORMER, Randy Hughson
THE PERFECTIONIST, Henry Czerny
THE PURITAN, R.H. Thomson

Liner Notes

This is a difficult play to convey on the page because the time-space conventions of theatre are in a constant state of flux. The central conceit is that we are inside Glenn Gould's head and anything is possible. Each character can invoke dimensional shifts, or be subject to dimensional shifts invoked by others. A few clarifying comments seem in order to ease the reader's journey:

The Goldberg Variations: Gould began and ended his recording career with Bach's Goldberg Variations. The play is divided into an opening Aria, thirty Variations and a Final Aria which, in most cases, follow the voicing, structure and mood prescribed in Bach's score. For example, if the Variation is an arabesque with two voices there are two characters in the scene; if the Variation is a canon then the two voices play a game of chase, and so on. The 'ground bass' mentioned in the stage directions refers to a thirty-two-note harmonic progression laid out in the Aria. Each of the Variations has its own independent character based on the harmonic implications of this ground bass. The end result is harmonic, rather than melodic, unity.

The Theatrical Score: Each Variation features recorded music culled from Glenn Gould's life in the studio. His early and late recordings of the Goldberg Variations receive prominent coverage, but the score draws liberally from his entire *oeuvre.* Since this excerpting of recorded material was being done at the time of publication specific musical choices are seldom noted in the stage directions. In some cases the recorded material is 'sampled' with technology—a musical phrase, looped, phased, compressed or extended to highlight some aspect of Gould's technique or the harmonic dimensions of the music itself. In most instances the music serves as a background wash, a kind of Gouldian wallpaper. From time to time the lights go out so that the audience can concentrate entirely on Gould's playing without visual distraction. *At no time does an actor sit at the keyboard and pretend to play one of Glenn Gould's recorded performances.*

Entrances and Exits: In most cases entrances and exits indicated in the stage directions refer to characters entering and leaving lighted playing areas. The characters rarely leave the stage entirely.

Furniture and Props: There are a number of chairs on-stage— Gould's legendary piano chair, a swivel chair in the recording studio, a plain chair which serves multiple functions and a La-Z-Boy at the family cottage at Uptergrove. A piano keyboard is suspended on wires throughout the play. At a couple of key moments a hanging piano harp drops into the action from above. There is a recording console with a telephone. All other props are carried on and off by the cast.

Other Dramatis Personae: 'Jessie' refers to Jessie Grieg, Glenn Gould's cousin and lifelong soul-mate. Jessie never appears on-stage in person. From time to time the four characters assume the guise of alter egos Glenn Gould developed in his humorous writings viz. Theodore Slutz, Wolfgang von Krankmeister etc. At other times they play real people like Herbert von Karajan, or invented characters like Mr. Ramsay or Larry Lewman. The convention here is one of gamesmanship and blatant role-playing. At no time does the audience lose sight of the Gouldian persona behind the mask.

At its premiere in Toronto the play was performed in the round.

ACT I

*As the audience enters an engineer is moving microphone
stands, positioning them around a piano keyboard that hangs
suspended on wires centre-stage. He listens under earphones
while he strikes notes we cannot hear on the keyboard. A bank
of reel-to-reel tape decks, mixing boards and other recording
paraphernalia are visually prominent behind a low console with
a swivel chair—the control console—off to one side. The rest of
the playing area is clean*

*Audience members start to settle when they realize that the
engineer has miked the hall and is feeding back tape-delays of
their ambient sound through a surround of speakers*

Lights fade

*As the lights come down a tape collage is added to the mix, fragments
of pre-recorded speculation about Glenn Gould. We listen to
on-the-street interviews from a range of age groups and ethnic
backgrounds. The question posed is: 'Tell me three things about
Glenn Gould.' The responses are discrete rather than overlapped*

VOICES [*a building crescendo*] … a famous pianist … dunked
his hands in this really hot … hat, scarf, gloves—does that
count for three? … quit performing … child prodigy … I
think he was part lizard … total hypochondriac … swear
you were looking at the young Bob Dylan … a hermit …
from the Beaches … this special stool … photographic memory
… night owl … the guy sneezes on the phone and Gould …
a monk … the singing … obsessed with technology …

drove around all night ... he took pills ... Fran's Restaurant
... pretty sure he was ... a recluse ... gay? ... a piano player,
right? ... a telephone addict ... hated the cold ... loved the
north ... the Goldbergs ... he was Jewish ... lived on
scrambled eggs ... this thing about solitude ... listen, I'm
going to have to call you right back. I've got Glenn Gould
on the other line—that's right, Glenn Gould!

[*The tape reaches peak volume, stops abruptly. Silence. A single
note call of a cardinal. The sound reverberates, fades down to
silence*]

ARIA

Lights up: The keyboard hangs suspended in space

Music up: Aria, late version

*A pair of white-gloved hands moves into the light from below
and begins to conduct. A voice hums low along with the music.
One by one other gloved hands enter the light to conduct the
music. With each new set of hands another Gould vocalizes
under the Aria—until eight hands are conducting music which
is almost entirely masked by Gouldian 'singing.' A sense of
disharmony and conflicting purpose*

Lights shift to reveal: THE PRODIGY, THE PERFORMER, THE
PERFECTIONIST *and* THE PURITAN. THE PERFORMER *and* THE
PERFECTIONIST *are like two opposing corner men preparing
their boys for a wrestling bout. There is an aggressive sense of
competition between the two handlers. They glare at each other
as they deliver last-minute instructions about fingering technique.* THE PURITAN *and* THE PRODIGY *face away from each
other, lost in private contemplation of their hands*

PERFORMER Physical space is an alluring distraction.
PERFECTIONIST Chronological time is a trap.
PERFORMER We are each our own creation.
PERFECTIONIST We will a world into being—
PERFORMER & PERFECTIONIST And fill it with—
PRODIGY & PURITAN Ourselves.

> [*Trainers remove coats and hats from 'the fighters' and with-
> draw into the shadows.* THE PRODIGY *and* THE PURITAN *turn
> toward each other for the first time. They do not make eye
> contact. Instead, they move to the other's corner ... and begin
> waltzing with imaginary partners. They dance until the Aria
> ends. Lights shift. The first note from the 'ground bass' sounds*]

VARIATION I: ECSTASY

THE PURITAN *moves toward the audience.* THE PRODIGY *goes
to a table, picks up a yellow legal-length pad and begins to write*

Music up: Variation 1, the early version

PURITAN I recently re-recorded the Goldberg Variations,
returning to Bach's text in my forty-eighth year. As a
prelude to the recording sessions I of course felt obliged to
listen to my original interpretation of the score which is now
some thirty-one years old ...

> [*Light on* THE PRODIGY, *who reads from his yellow legal-length
> pad.* THE PURITAN *is turned away from him. They remain
> unaware of one another*]

PRODIGY [*reading from his pad*] Letter to posterity. I am about
to record the Goldberg Variations. I spent this morning
going over the score and for the first time I could hear the

entire thing in my head.

PURITAN & PRODIGY [*in unison*] It was a spooky experience.

[*They are both startled by the echo effect. They don't look at each other*]

PRODIGY I felt as if I was standing outside myself, listening with my inner ear to music I was born to play ...

PURITAN My first impression was that there was quite a bit of piano playing on that record, and I mean that in the most derogatory sense possible. Strangely, I could not recognize or identify with the spirit of the person who made that recording.

PRODIGY I felt like I was listening to someone else ...

[*Lights up: on* THE PERFECTIONIST, *sitting at his control console. He turns up the volume on the early version of Variation 1*]

And the music he was playing! I was ... transported!

[THE PRODIGY *begins to move in a rhapsodic dance*]

PURITAN The condition of ecstasy is a kind of standing apart from the self. I have spent my life trying to sustain that moment of rapturous transcendence.

PRODIGY The music carrying me up and up and up!

PURITAN When the world is young, ecstasy is a kind of sensual drunkenness. You rush around after it, exhilarated by the happy accidents and disorders of intuition.

[THE PERFECTIONIST *cross-fades to the late version of Variation 1.* THE PRODIGY *pauses in his rhapsodic dance, considering the slower tempo*]

Years of sober reflection bring a deeper understanding and the ecstasy of youth becomes yet another thing to be transcended—

PRODIGY I remember where all of this began. Those Sunday afternoon drives home from Lake Simcoe when I first learned to listen ...

PURITAN In maturity, ecstasy becomes a kind of … inconsolable longing.

PRODIGY Grey light fading into grey land. February in Ontario. Bare trees in patches. A farmhouse with one light on, the pond scraped clean where kids were skating.

[THE PERFECTIONIST *cross-fades to the early version of Variation 1*]

PURITAN One longs to be part of some larger unity. The moment bursting forth. 'All the bells that ever rung still ringing in the long, dying light.'

PRODIGY Mother tunes in the New York Philharmonic on the CBC. The music swells to fill the car … rings harmonics in my inner ear …

[THE PERFECTIONIST *mixes both versions of Variation 1*]

The music coming to life inside my head! Me playing it all!

[THE PRODIGY *conducts the music he's hearing in his head*]

PURITAN I sense that I am entering a period of great change. A new beginning, really … as I cross this threshold into the unknown I must remember everything I ever knew about bravery … in such moments, one cocks an ear toward the past … one *listens*.

[*Both versions of Variation 1 end together*]

PRODIGY I am Busoni! And Bach never sounded so good!

[THE PURITAN *and* THE PRODIGY *exit without connecting.* THE PERFECTIONIST *moves from behind his console. Lights shift. The second note from the ground bass sounds*]

VARIATION 2: THE IVORY TOWER

THE PERFECTIONIST *cues the engineer. A red lightbulb which stands in for the camera blinks on.* THE PERFECTIONIST *addresses it as he moves around the control console*

PERFECTIONIST Take-twoness. If you don't understand the concept of take-twoness you'll never understand me. I mean, really, who is to say that on *this* night at *this particular* piano we are going to hear *this* performer's definitive rendering of the work in question? The odds are against it, so I moved on. It's here in the studio, with the technical potential offered by many takes, many discrete creative decisions, where the artist can truly make works of transcendental significance ...

[THE PERFECTIONIST *sits down in a swivel chair in front of the 'camera'*]

Embracing that recognition, I withdrew from the concert stage some fifteen years ago and began to make controversial public pronouncements about the future of serious music. Not surprisingly, the critics came after me with torches and pitchforks. [*pausing to dab his forehead with a finger*] Stop tape. We're glistening.

[THE PERFECTIONIST *pats his face dry with a handkerchief. The red light blinks off.* THE PRODIGY *rushes out and pours a bag of dominoes on the stage.* THE PURITAN *enters talking on the telephone. Music up: Scoring based on Variation 2. As* THE PRODIGY *counts out his dominoes he sings the notes of the bass line*]

PRODIGY [*under other dialogue*] One, two, three, four, five, six, seven, eight, nine, ten, eleven, twelve, thirteen, fourteen, fifteen, sixteen, seventeen, eighteen, nineteen, twenty,

twenty-one, twenty-two, twenty-three, twenty-four, twenty-five, twenty-six, twenty-seven, twenty-eight, twenty-nine, thirty, thirty-one, thirty-two.

PURITAN Just a minute, Susan, my cousin Jessie is here and I want her to ... repeat that last part. [*to Jessie; addressing an empty chair*] The *New York Times* review.

[THE PRODIGY *finishes counting out the dominoes, pulls out a bag of candy Love Hearts and shakes one loose. He reads the phrase written on it*]

PRODIGY 'Love you forever.'

[*He thinks about eating it, then puts it away*]

PURITAN [*on phone*] 'The new Goldbergs are less viscerally intoxicating ... but more affecting. More *serious*. More seductive in their depth ...' [*to Jessie*] Who should be hearing this right now, Jessie?

PRODIGY Mother!

[THE PRODIGY *begins putting dominoes on end in a large arc, counting as he goes*]

[*under*] Aria, One. Two. One, two, three.

[THE PERFECTIONIST *cues the engineer. The red light blinks on and he re-addresses himself to it*]

PERFECTIONIST [*adjusting his posture*] How was I? Like this? Fine. Let's move on. [*host mode*] Criticism and Labels. Early on in my performing career I discovered that the gladitorial element inherent in the concert situation encouraged the worst tendencies in the musical press.

[THE PERFECTIONIST *allows space for the others to speak. He's in control of the proceedings here*]

PURITAN [*into phone*] What was that last bit? [*repeating to Jessie*]

'The contemplative meditation of the Aria, the splendid
varieties of attack in the fifteenth Variation ...' [*cupping the
receiver*] It gets better, Jessie.

PERFECTIONIST Instead of retreating into the rapturous state of
innerness which *real listening* engenders, the critics kept their
eyes wide open and saw a man in ill-fitting evening wear
conducting himself at the keyboard.

PRODIGY [*still placing dominoes; under*] One, two, three. One,
two, three. One, two, three. One.

PERFECTIONIST [*quoting*] 'Mr. Gould waving to and fro on his
pygmy piano stool affects strange mannerisms ... conducting himself with his free hand ... singing along with his
performance ... all these affectations work to his own
detriment.' One might have expected that after I retired
from the 'pro tour' the critics would have found something
else to talk about.

PURITAN [*relaying to Jessie*] '... the detached and crystalline
character of the epic twenty-fifth ... the almost frightening
clarity in the virtuosic parts ...'

PERFECTIONIST No such luck. 'In his most recent recordings of
Mozart, Mr. Gould continues to show an unrepentant desire
to shock the grown-ups.'

PRODIGY Mother!

PERFECTIONIST Well, let me assure you, by now I've read *all*
the labels: 'Gould the Philosopher King.'

PURITAN [*relaying to Jessie*] '... create a Goldberg that gives
both a sense of ecstasy ... and of quiet repose.' And who
should be hearing this?

PRODIGY Mother!

PERFECTIONIST 'Gould the Recluse.'

PURITAN Susan, thanks so much for calling this in. Yes. Indeed.
Perhaps someday soon we'll have an opportunity to meet
face to face— [*he hangs up*] —but don't bet on it. Well,
Jessie, it certainly was a wonderful review. This critic

understood, but I'm not about to take it deeply to heart.

PERFECTIONIST 'Gould the Neurotic Wreck.'

PURITAN [*to Jessie*] Sunday painters believe their reviews.

PERFECTIONIST 'Gould the Control Freak.'

PRODIGY [*under*] Mother! Two, three. One, two, three. One, two, three. One. Two, three. One. Two, three. One-two, three. Aria.

PERFECTIONIST 'Gould the Stoic.'

PURITAN [*to Jessie*] It's a bit late in the day for the musical press to be doing me any favours.

PERFECTIONIST 'Gould the Sexual Enigma.'

[THE PRODIGY *contemplates the arc of dominoes he has assembled*]

PRODIGY Ahhh, so *beautiful.*

PERFECTIONIST 'Gould the Self-Mythologizer.'

PURITAN Jessie, I know the story they want to tell: The eccentric piano virtuoso, now paunchy and grey of skin, goes back to re-record the work that established him as a young artist.

PRODIGY [*points at first domino*] Aria.

PURITAN The theme-and-variation of the music a template for the arc of the performer's life—the melodic figurations of early genius transformed by the burdens of age—

PRODIGY [*points at seventeenth domino*] French Overture.

PURITAN … all of it supposedly there in Bach's text.

PRODIGY The twenty-fifth Variation.

PERFECTIONIST 'Gould the Vaudevillian.'

PURITAN I can hear Herr von Hockmeister now: [*German accent*] 'Zer could be no more meaningful *mise en scène* against vich to offset Mr. Gould's hermetic lifestyle and his continuing quest for autobiographical martyrdom.'

PERFECTIONIST 'Gould the Technological Quack.'

PRODIGY [*points at second-last domino*] Quodlibet.

PURITAN Pardon?

PERFECTIONIST 'Gould the Pharmaceutical Enthusiast.'

[THE PRODIGY *fishes another candy Love Heart out of the bag, reads it, then pops it in his mouth*]

PRODIGY 'You're the one.'

[*A beeper goes off on* THE PURITAN*'s watch. He pushes a button to silence it. Retrieves a vial of pills from his coat pocket, shakes one loose and swallows it. Takes his own pulse. All of this is very routine*]

PERFECTIONIST 'Gould the Hypochondriac.'

[THE PRODIGY *sings the notes of the bass line. Very fast*]

PURITAN I am taking care of myself, Jessie. I've been working eighteen hours a day in Manhattan. I should look even worse.

PRODIGY [*points at last domino*] Aria. [*exiting*] Mother! I've figured out the Goldbergs!

PERFECTIONIST The funny thing about this proliferation of labels is that none of them properly identifies the real Glenn Gould.

[THE PERFECTIONIST *stands.* THE PRODIGY*'s domino array is spread at his feet.* THE PERFECTIONIST *tromps through them, unaware*]

PURITAN I know you're worried, Jessie. So am I. I've always *been* worried. [*he looks at his hands for a long moment*] All of this is borrowed.

[THE PURITAN *turns away from Jessie's chair and goes to pick up the dominoes. SFX: Arctic wind. Lights shift. The third note from the ground bass sounds*]

VARIATION 3: THE POLAR SEA VS. RED

Cross-fade to: Sounds of orchestra tuning up. THE PERFORMER
paces on-stage. He's wound very tight. He takes his own pulse

PERFORMER Borderline eurythmia.

[THE PERFORMER *takes a pill.* THE PURITAN *finishes collecting
the dominoes and moves into shadow.* THE PERFORMER *paces
and conducts himself, trying to concentrate on the unheard
music.* THE PRODIGY *moves to sit in front of Jessie's chair with a
typewriter on his knee.* THE PERFECTIONIST *sidles up beside*
THE PERFORMER]

PERFECTIONIST Ready to play?
PERFORMER I will be playing, in about five minutes—
PERFECTIONIST I mean, the game.
PERFORMER You never get tired of it, do you?
PERFECTIONIST Fish swim. Birds fly. I play the game. And this
is a canon.
PERFORMER [*sardonic*] Well then, I suppose I could give you a run.
PERFECTIONIST I was thinking more along the lines of a
lightening fast encirclement.
PERFORMER Ho-ho, aren't we robust this evening—
PERFECTIONIST Indeed. Got someone in mind?
PERFORMER I don't know. Let me see ...

[THE PERFORMER *turns in a slow, deliberate circle, conducting
with little gestures of one hand. He holds finger to temple*]

PERFECTIONIST You always do that when you're trying to know.
PERFORMER I don't *try to* know, my friend. I *know.*

[THE PRODIGY *stops typing. He's in a foul mood*]

PRODIGY *Mother* thinks she knows and she doesn't, Jessie.
That's the problem. When I say I know, I *know.* When she

says she knows she only *thinks* she knows.

[THE PURITAN *enters. He is invisible to the other players*]

PERFORMER [*throwing down the gauntlet*] Okay. I've got someone. Go ahead.

PERFECTIONIST Someone I've met?

PRODIGY Have you listened to the way she talks? There should be a roadside shrine!

[THE PURITAN *homes in on* THE PRODIGY. THE PRODIGY *is unaware of his presence*]

PERFORMER Someone you've met and would like to know better.

PRODIGY [*parroting his mother*] I always wanted a classical pianist. I played music all the time I was carrying him and prayed for a gift from God.

PERFECTIONIST Hm.

PRODIGY [*mother's voice*] When he was an infant he'd sit on my knee at the piano and hit a single note with one finger. Then he'd listen until the sound had entirely faded away ... *fish wrap.* [*indicating his typing*] If she knew what I was doing in here she'd go *mental.*

[THE PRODIGY *resumes his feverish two-finger typing.* THE PURITAN *reads over his shoulder*]

She makes me see red, Jessie. And that's *dangerous.*

PERFECTIONIST This person you're thinking of—if she were a body of water which body of water would she be?

PERFORMER Did I say this person was a 'she'?

PERFECTIONIST Water is always feminine.

[THE PRODIGY *rolls the sheet up in his typewriter so that he can read to Jessie*]

PRODIGY Special to the *Daily Woof.* 'Mozart Sez: Fungus Amungus!' [*he goes back to furious typing*]

PERFORMER I'd be the Polar Sea.

[*The words 'Polar Sea' spark* THE PURITAN*'s interest. He approaches* THE PERFORMER *and* THE PERFECTIONIST]

PERFECTIONIST A-ha. The feminine principle embedded in a barren landscape. Interesting paradox.

[*A painful chord sounds.* THE PURITAN *feels a sting of pain, looks up, seeking the source*]

PRODIGY [*calling out*] G Diminished Seventh ... Mother! [*reading to Jessie*] Mozart the budgie has come down with an under-feather fungus. According to the budgie: [*Mozart voice*] 'It is da constant battle for control in da Gould household which has lead to my skin eruptions. Glenn and his mother can't decide who is da boss ...'

[*Another chord sounds. More pain for* THE PURITAN]

[*calling out*] E! A! B-flat! C! F! Major and minor seconds sandwiched between perfect fourths! I'm not slouching! [*reading, Mozart voice*] 'Young Mr. Gould is currently banished to his room and forbidden to touch da piano until further notice— [*calling out*] Mother? Please? [*to himself*] Who cares about stupid report cards?

PERFECTIONIST Would you more often be stormy or calm?

PERFORMER Given the right conditions I can be very, very stormy. And when I'm stormy, watch out.

PRODIGY [*as he types*] I'm serious, Jessie, I could kill her.

PERFECTIONIST [*reacting to* THE PRODIGY] Hostile!

PERFORMER Remote, not hostile.

PRODIGY [*interrupting her*] Jessie, I *see* red, but I'm not temperamentally inclined to *act* red. [*he continues his typing*]

PERFECTIONIST Most people think of the Polar Sea as hostile.

PERFORMER The Polar Sea is a paradox—hostile, yet *brimming* with life. To understand her is to become a philosopher.

PRODIGY I'm a prisoner, Jessie …

[*The word 'prisoner' sparks* THE PURITAN*'s interest. He returns his attention to* THE PRODIGY]

PERFECTIONIST An explorer in the thrall of the Great Unknown?
PERFORMER In seeking truth we become part of the truth we seek. That is an official clue.
PERFECTIONIST The anthropic principle?
PERFORMER Precisely. The human mind cannot escape the web of its own thinking.

[*Another chord. Another shot of pain for* THE PURITAN]

PRODIGY [*to mother*] G! C-sharp! D! G-sharp! The intervalus diabolus, two of them! Separated by a minor second! [*to Jessie*] I *hate* this stupid game. Mother?
PERFECTIONIST Werner Heisenberg.
PERFORMER Wrong side of the brain.
PRODIGY I swear to you, some day I'm going to look back on this day, Jessie …

[THE PURITAN *is close to* THE PRODIGY *now, hanging on his every word*]

… I'm going to remember it as the day … I decided to …
PERFECTIONIST I'm in a box canyon here.
PRODIGY —to escape. I'm going to chart my own course.
PERFORMER Think 'horizon line.' When you look into my eyes you feel like you can see forever.
PERFECTIONIST Barbra Streisand?
PERFORMER Wrong side of the galaxy. Imagine an outpouring of emotion that's cool to the touch.
PERFECTIONIST *Streisand!* What's your problem?

[THE PRODIGY *stands*]

PRODIGY [*holding up his two hands*] *This* is all I own, Jessie.

I can't expect others to understand.

PERFECTIONIST Scriabin.

PERFORMER [*smile*] No, but he did write the soundtrack for the region.

PRODIGY [*to himself*] Every escape begins with … one … small … step.

[THE PRODIGY *stands, hesitating, looking off toward his mother*]

PERFECTIONIST I'm going nowhere!

PRODIGY Mother? I *apologize*, okay?

[THE PRODIGY *exits*]

PERFECTIONIST Pardon my moment of pique. Let's try another tack. If this person were a chair, what kind of chair would he be?

PERFORMER Are chairs male?

PERFECTIONIST Usually.

PERFORMER I'd be … an uncomfortable throne.

[THE PURITAN *slowly sits down on the chair. Lights fade. The fourth note from the ground bass sounds*]

VARIATION 4: CREATIVE DECEPTION

THE PURITAN *sits alone on his uncomfortable throne*

THE PERFECTIONIST *enters and sits in front of the camera.* THE PURITAN *watches him closely.* THE PERFECTIONIST *is unaware of* THE PURITAN

PURITAN Studio G in the CBC building on Jarvis Street—my beautiful prison. I spent thousands of hours in this room fabricating a certain kind of truth. I ruled here like a Roman emperor, building great aqueducts for the sound of myself.

[THE PERFECTIONIST *cues his engineer. The red light blinks on*]

PERFECTIONIST [*to camera*] To understand the biographer's art one must first understand how disparate eras cohere, and that means understanding the splice.

PURITAN [*refuting him*] Most biographers are forgers, forever trying to situate their heroes slightly in advance of the nearest historically significant movement.

PERFECTIONIST Take Manhattan and put it alongside your mother's living room in the Beaches.

PURITAN Glenn Gould, Canadian child prodigy, is discovered in New York City and catapulted to worldwide fame. It's too easy!

PERFECTIONIST With a single jump-cut the biographer spans a decade.

PURITAN And misses the truth.

PERFECTIONIST Let's have a little fun. What we're after here is the contrapuntal relationships between psyche and era. A new way to eavesdrop on the self ...

PURITAN The process of *becoming* within the individual psyche is unconscious, indeterminate and wholly subliminal—each *day* a new era.

[THE PERFECTIONIST *is on his feet, moved by the energy of his own story*]

PERFECTIONIST First splice. Midtown Manhattan, 1955.

PURITAN Warp Eight, Scotty ...

[*Soundtrack: Big city ambience, traffic, horns, etc.* THE PRODIGY *enters wearing overcoat, cap, muffler and gloves*]

PRODIGY Taxi!

[THE PRODIGY *gets into a cab*]

PERFECTIONIST My first impression was that New Yorkers were

larger than life—flamboyant, exuberant!

PRODIGY Columbia Masterworks, two-oh-seven East Thirty Street.

PURITAN They looked at the world and saw only themselves.

PRODIGY [*leaning forward to answer a question*] Toronto, actually. That's in Canada. Everybody up there dresses like this in June.

PERFECTIONIST There was this one fellow, Larry Lewman. Larry was a techie in the Columbia Masterworks Studio on 30th … this kind of guy …

[THE PERFECTIONIST *physicalizes into a New York slouch*]

PURITAN And so the creative deception begins …

PERFECTIONIST [*as* LARRY LEWMAN] I worked with all the greats over the years, Horowitz, Schnabel, Cassals—I mean, I *know* classical musicians are quirky types—but nothing prepared me for this kid. He's from Canader, right? He arrives midtown with our address on a matchbook cover and ten bucks in his pocket. The ten spot's got a moose where George Washington's supposed to be. Anyway, he loses the address and arrives an hour late for the session. [*out of character*] In fact, I think I was an hour early.

PURITAN I was an hour late. I'd been walking the streets alone, summoning my courage, intensely aware that one era of my life was about to end so another could begin. [*to* LARRY] He invents what he needs and calls it the truth.

[THE PRODIGY *enters the Columbia recording studio and begins to lay out his supplies on a low table—Poland water, a pile of manuscripts, a tackle box full of vitamins*]

LARRY He saunters into the studio, it's June, right, it's eighty-five degrees, for crissakes, and he's dressed for a blizzard! The next thing, he starts in with this kooky chair—it's a bridge chair, basically, which his dad made for him up in

Canader. Collapsible. Screw fittings on the legs. Weird. He works on it—Minnesota Fats assembling a cue.

[THE PURITAN *realizes his chair is slightly off-balance. He makes minor adjustments*]

LARRY Then he asks for a basin of hot water, make it scalding he says. The kid rolls up his sleeves and puts his arms in up to here.
PRODIGY Anybody else find it a little cool in here?

[THE PRODIGY *soaks his arms. He's feeling very vulnerable in this moment*]

LARRY This is the best part. It's a stinking hot June day, he's got his arms in boiling water and he's asking us to turn off the air conditioning!
PRODIGY [*proud smile*] I have borderline tracheitis.

[THE PURITAN *positions his perfected chair by the keyboard.* THE PRODIGY *moves toward it.* THE PERFORMER *comes on-stage, stands outside the action, watching carefully*]

LARRY So we're thinking, uh-oh, call Bellevue, but then he sits down at the piano …

[THE PRODIGY *moves toward the keyboard,* THE PERFORMER *slips past him and takes the chair, raises his hands to play. Everyone goes into a freeze. Snap to black. We listen in the dark while Glenn Gould plays a blindingly brilliant passage. Lights up:* THE PRODIGY *is nowhere to be seen.* THE PERFORMER *gets up from the piano very slowly, coming back to himself by degrees*]

PERFORMER Or something like that—

[*It takes* THE PERFECTIONIST *and* THE PURITAN *a moment to re-focus*]

LARRY So anyway, I turn to him and I say: The twenty-fifth Variation, kid. You crawled through it! What gives?

PERFORMER Everything generates out of the Aria—this little ground bass line that is duplicated and re-duplicated in the Variations.

LARRY Hey, I know the score! [*he sings the first notes of the bass line*] What's that got to do with playing the twenty-fifth so slow?

PERFORMER Think architecture. The Aria and the first two Variations at the beginning. The two penultimate Variations and the Quodlibet at the end. Framed between these two support structures, Variations are grouped like the interior columns of a baroque church. Everything in threes. First, a canon: intense contrapuntal games, question and answer, theme chasing theme. Second: an independent Variation darting this way and that like a hummingbird. And, last but not least, the sinuous dance of a two-manual arabesque. And there's your structure.

LARRY But the twenty-fifth—so help me God, you *crawled* through it!

PERFORMER You're not inside it yet. Eight of these three-member units between the opening and closing. One in three and three in one. Does that suggest anything to you?

LARRY A club sandwich?

PERFORMER The Holy Trinity embedded in a sacred architecture of sound! Pattern and control in the service of spiritual ecstasy, that's the *essence* of Bach!

LARRY You're a beat poet. Go daddy-o!

PERFORMER The sublime paradox is that the physical reality of this music has, what, a momentary existence in the mind of the listener? It's a means of communicating the mysteries of the sacred in a form which is equally mysterious, and therefore equally sacred.

LARRY Beautiful. Now, why is the twenty-fifth so slow?

PERFORMER What's gone before? A processional of songs, dances, declamations and meditations has carried us deep into Bach's cathedral. Now, with the twenty-fifth, we are

granted a pause, an opportunity to cast our eyes up to the
rose window and meditate upon the larger mysteries. There's
no such thing as 'going too slow' in a moment like that.

LARRY Okay, I buy it, but—

PERFORMER [*interrupting*] Wait, my friend, this is a spiritual
journey. [*New Yorkese*] 'It ain't over till it's over.' Five more
Variations and then the Aria repeats—a suggestion of
perpetuity. There's a sense that this music has neither end
nor beginning, neither climax nor resolution. Like
Baudelaire's lovers, the composition—

PURITAN & PERFORMER '… rests lightly on the wings of the
unchecked wind.'

[THE PERFORMER *double-takes.* THE PERFECTIONIST *is shaken.*
THE PURITAN *approaches the scene with new interest, moving
close to* THE PERFORMER]

PERFORMER We are looking at nothing less than the marriage
of music, mathematics and metaphysics … at transcendence
itself.

LARRY Which is why you like the Goldbergs, this obscure piece
of music that …

PERFORMER [*interrupting*] Don't we all want to defy death?

LARRY You're too young to know anything about death.

PERFORMER It's in this room with us—one breath away.

[THE PURITAN *is startled. He looks at his hands with great sadness*]

LARRY You're a looney-tune, kid. I like that. You're gonna love
living down here.

PERFORMER Live here? No thanks. I prefer Lake Simcoe.

LARRY Lake Simcoe?

PERFORMER The Canadian outback. The wild frontier. That's
my home.

[LARRY *does a take on that*]

LARRY You're pulling my leg.

PERFORMER Quite the contrary, I can walk out the back door of my cabin and go two thousand miles straight north without encountering another human being. Growing up alongside that fact does something to the architecture of thought itself. Bach would have loved the high Arctic.

LARRY I'd be scared shitless.

[THE PERFORMER *is at a loss for words*]

PURITAN You'd be less certain of your importance.

LARRY What you want to bet you'll end up in Manhattan?

PERFORMER I'll bet you ... my life.

[*Lights fade. The fifth note from the ground bass sounds*]

VARIATION 5: FISH AND FISHERMAN

SFX: Bird calls. The single piercing note of a cardinal

Lights up on a rowboat. THE PURITAN *is on board, casting for bass. He has a pork-pie fishing hat pulled down over his eyes— an awkward attempt at disguise.* THE PRODIGY *enters*

PRODIGY My mother and father worry that somehow the world will steal my childhood. That's why dad bought this cottage up on Lake Simcoe. It's my refuge. A place for me to connect with the important stuff ... trees ... birds ...

[THE PURITAN *casts his line with a zing*]

Bass fishing. Even here in paradise I am aware of a degree of separation. Others don't feel what I am feeling, [*stepping into the boat*] take Mr. Ramsay, our neighbour. Mr. Ramsay is a simple man with a narrow range of emotional responses.

PURITAN [*as* MR. RAMSAY] Keep the tip moving, Professor.
Gotta keep it moving. That's it. You want to fool that fish.
Are you on bottom? [*he intercedes with* THE PRODIGY*'s fishing
technique*] You want the fish to think the worm is alive.

PRODIGY Mr. Ramsay has taken it upon himself to provide me
with some of the trappings of a normal childhood. The Dog
Paddle. The Sheep Shank. The dramaturgy of worms. He
calls me 'The Professor.'

[THE PRODIGY*'s fishing rod quivers*]

[*terrified whisper*] Oh no. Think I got a nibble.

MR. RAMSAY [*whisper*] He's gumming it. Don't move. [*he tests
the line with a finger*] You moved.

PRODIGY Mr. Ramsay and I play our little game. He puts a
worm on my hook. I play out my line until I feel the worm
settle on bottom. I don't want to fool the fish. I want to fool
Mr. Ramsay. [*pause*] I stare at the distant shore and *listen* …

[MR. RAMSAY *turns to listen, momentarily out of character as he
eavesdrops on the boy*]

I'm inside Bach's music so much of the time now. I open a
new score and the possibilities flash by me like dazzling
lures— *Zing! Zing!*

[MR. RAMSAY *casts with a loud zing. Continues his eavesdropping*]

I turn each new piece of music around in my head for days,
structure moving like the shapes of a mobile as I assemble the
unities … this emotion against that tempo! This wind against
that light! The symmetries ring harmonics deep into my
dreams, a call heard in the sleeping blood. [*in wonder*]
I converse with the dead. A joyous whispering of secrets. [*pause*]
I want to be the greatest interpreter of Bach since Busoni.

[*SFX: The call of a cardinal. The twang of a breaking piano string. The beep of a life-support system. The sound effect is terrifying—a feeling of lost balance, of falling off a cliff into empty space. This sound cluster hereafter referred to as 'the fish sting.' Light shift: To red.* THE PRODIGY'*s rod bends double, line races off his reel*]

Something is happening!

[MR. RAMSAY *is out of his depth here. He's never caught a fish either*]

MR. RAMSAY My goodness! Oh my goodness! Reel in! No! The other way! Look out, he's running! Let the drag off! THE DRAG!

PRODIGY Stop! Just do—any!—stop! It's-it's wrong! I-I won't be part of it!

PURITAN [*out of character*] You *are* part of it!

[*Pandemonium as the fish breaks water in a blaze of light and sound, then lands on the floorboards of the boat between them. SFX: Fish thumping against boat.* THE PURITAN *goes into a horrified freeze.* THE PRODIGY *steps away from the boat, trying to escape*]

PRODIGY I see everything from the fish's point of view—its entire being this single glittering muscle. It flops on the floor-boards—a fast cadence changing time in sporadic shudders ... the fish drowning in my air ... the movement becomes legato, soft little thumps ... as the sparkle dulls ... fades ... disappears. Dead eyes. Scales gone white. Silence ...

PURITAN ... and me screaming at the top of my lungs.

[THE PURITAN *comes out of his freeze. Looks at his hands. They are trembling with fear. He clenches them slowly into fists, looks at* THE PRODIGY *who stands nearby, caught up in his own grief.* THE PURITAN *takes a pill, backs slowly away into shadow. Lights fade. The sixth note from the ground bass sounds*]

VARIATION 6: TURNING AWAY

Music up: Scriabin

THE PERFORMER *and* THE PERFECTIONIST *enter.* THE PRODIGY *stands off to one side, facing away from them, still recovering from the horror of his fishing expedition*

PERFECTIONIST The uncomfortable throne, the hostile ocean that brims with life, the mind caught in the net of its own thinking— I have another line of questioning.
PERFORMER Play ball.

[THE PURITAN *enters carrying a baseball and glove. He is still shaken by events in the previous Variation. He moves toward* THE PRODIGY, *looking for an opening.* THE PERFECTIONIST *and* THE PERFORMER *carry on unaware*]

PERFECTIONIST If this person ran for office.
PERFORMER Sorry, I don't run. It's against my nature.
PERFECTIONIST Not a political bone in your body?
PERFORMER Indirect questions only, please.

[THE PURITAN *thwacks ball into glove.* THE PRODIGY *turns, sees* THE PURITAN *for the first time*]

PURITAN You're Glenn Gould, the piano player.
PRODIGY I am. And who are you?
PURITAN Larry. I coach little league over at the park. The Cardinals. The lads talk about you.
PRODIGY I'll bet they do.
PERFECTIONIST Let me put it this way then, if I were a political figure with whom our mystery guest *identified* ...?
PURITAN It must be pretty rough.
PRODIGY What do you mean?
PERFORMER Okay, I'll just say it. Ghandi.
PURITAN I hear they call you 'Ears.'

PERFECTIONIST [*thinking*] Ghandi. Ghandi. Nice clue.

PRODIGY I-I have rather prominent ears.

PERFORMER Think about what he lived face to face with.

PURITAN I told them you were brave. For trying to do what you're trying to do.

PERFECTIONIST Death. Ghandi lived face to face with death.

PRODIGY Brave people stand in front of bullets. I'm afraid that's not my style.

[THE PRODIGY *turns away from* THE PURITAN *again.* THE PURITAN *bangs ball into mitt, waiting for another opening*]

PERFORMER Now examine if you will his vocabulary of responses to that situation. Good gracious, why am I giving you all these clues?

PERFECTIONIST Your insatiable need to please. The Performer's perversity.

PERFORMER A perversity which you have relinquished, I suppose ...

PERFECTIONIST A perversity which I have learned to transcend ...

PURITAN Have you told your mother you're quitting school?

PRODIGY Who said I was quitting school?

PURITAN My ... ah ... my shortstop.

PERFECTIONIST ... let me see, Ghandi's response to death ...

[THE PRODIGY *turns half around*]

PRODIGY I-I'm thinking about it.

PERFECTIONIST Passive resistance!

PURITAN Are you frightened?

PRODIGY Why all these questions?

PURITAN Animal curiosity. I'd like to know ... what you know.

PRODIGY I-I see no reason for fear.

PURITAN It's a big world out there. You only have Grade Eleven.

PRODIGY I have ... other things.

[*He turns away again*]

PERFECTIONIST [*thinking*] An uncomfortable throne. A hostile ocean that brims with life. A pacifist politician. Beware, my friend, the tumblers have begun to click ...

[THE PERFECTIONIST *turns away from* THE PERFORMER, *conducting and thinking*]

PURITAN But will what you have be enough?
PRODIGY What do you mean?
PURITAN So much can happen in a life. Will what you have sustain you over the long journey?
PERFORMER [*taunting*] Click. Click.
PRODIGY I-I can't answer that question.
PURITAN You must.
PRODIGY Why?
PURITAN Because ... because ... it's hard to describe—it's ...

[THE PURITAN *also begins to conduct himself, thinking.* THE PERFECTIONIST *faces* THE PERFORMER *with new assurance*]

PERFECTIONIST I *see* you. The game is the lens of my camera.

[THE PERFECTIONIST *and* THE PERFORMER *move eyeball to eyeball*]

Click.
PURITAN [*finding the words*] —it's that you'll look back on these days for the rest of your life. You're setting a personal standard for bravery.
PRODIGY Sir, I am not brave. I'm even afraid of that baseball ...
PERFECTIONIST [*musing*] You're afraid of me, aren't you?
PURITAN [*extending the ball and glove*] Catching it with the bare hands?
PERFORMER Hardly ...
PRODIGY I've never done it.
PURITAN Really, quite horrifying. I've never done it either.

PRODIGY I thought you said you coached.

PURITAN I do. It's ... it's my way of addressing the fear.

PERFECTIONIST Raw, animal fear. [*turning away from* THE PERFORMER] You can't fool me. You have been seen.

PURITAN Want to have a go?

PRODIGY I suppose I should be able to say I once caught a ball.

PURITAN It would be nice, just once, to throw one.

[THE PURITAN *winds up. Ready to throw.* THE PRODIGY *holds out his hands. Both of them are afraid.* THE PERFECTIONIST *wheels around*]

PERFECTIONIST Okay, high fast ball. Lenny Bernstein.

PERFORMER Bernstein? Why Bernstein?

PERFECTIONIST Lenny is a pacifist who'd never run for office. I saw him run for a cab once. Not pretty.

PERFORMER I'm going to give you a huge clue. I want you to think about it before we play the game again.

[THE PURITAN *and* THE PRODIGY *are still trying to throw the ball. It's agonizing*]

'Transcending human experience.'

[THE PURITAN *throws a feeble dribbler—they both turn away. The ball misses* THE PRODIGY *entirely. They turn slowly toward one another—is it over yet?*]

PERFECTIONIST Transcending human experience ...

PRODIGY Does that count?

PURITAN Of course it counts.

PRODIGY Nice talking to you ...

PURITAN Where you headed?

PRODIGY North.

PURITAN Godspeed ...

[*Lights fade. The seventh note from the ground bass sounds*]

VARIATION 7: TURNING TOWARD

PURITAN —my first bold move away from the world of everyday routine. In 1952 I dropped out of high school, ended my
piano lessons with Mr. Guerrero and went to Uptergrove,
the family cottage on Lake Simcoe.

[THE PRODIGY *enters and paces around a telephone, trying to
decide if he should make a call*]

I remember going to great lengths to be alone on my birthday.

[THE PRODIGY *picks up the phone. Dials a couple of digits.
Hangs up again*]

PRODIGY The twenty-fifth of September. No cake. No candles.
No celebration. Instead this ... this inconsolable longing.

PURITAN It was a test. A chance to look at myself on the barren
heath, so to speak.

PRODIGY I feel like I'm circling above my childhood, never
finding a place to land except ...

[THE PRODIGY *moves toward the phone again. Should he call?*]

PURITAN [*gaining conviction*] The idea of solitude was with me
from the very beginning. Isolation was a doorway to ecstasy.

[THE PRODIGY *moves away from the phone*]

PRODIGY ... except in this ... this condition of solitary con-
finement. The contradiction pulls at me.

PURITAN That recognition gave me strength—a raw certainty
that empowered every conscious decision.

PRODIGY I arrive in the place where I most want to be and my
only thought is of escape. [*he looks at the phone*] I've taken
myself prisoner.

PURITAN Solitude was to be the great connector for all the convic-
tions that followed. The air lock between behaviour and belief.

PRODIGY If I feed that way of thinking it will surely destroy me. I must embrace the separation I feel and *build* on it. But how?

[THE PRODIGY *closes his eyes. Gestures toward a grand possibility. This gesture hereafter known as 'taking flight'*]

Imagine a house on stilts, the treetops are laid at my feet like a nubbly lawn. Clouds bend around the bowl of the sky. The earth is the crown of my head.

[*Music up: Variation 7, early version.* THE PERFECTIONIST *enters to his work area behind the console and is surprised to discover the moment-in-progress between* THE PURITAN *and* THE PRODIGY. *He pays keen attention*]

PURITAN Solitude whets the appetite for mastering challenges. It puts iron in the soul ...

PRODIGY [*opening his eyes*] I am atop the first tree I ever climbed. It's still my favourite. No one knows I come here—they think I'm not the tree-climbing type.

PURITAN ... and gives a personal definition to heroism.

PRODIGY The danger is an aspect of the euphoria I feel, up as high as I can go ... on the outer edge of control ...

PURITAN Those months at Uptergrove were a kind of mental training ground—

PRODIGY ... holding tight when a sudden gust of wind snaps the leaves around me pale green ...

PURITAN By the time my sojourn was over I was equipped for a career on the concert stage ...

PRODIGY ... the whole world rocks back and forth, my heart with it!

PURITAN ... my feelings about the world had been annealed by the fires of isolation!

[*SFX: The single note of a cardinal's song*]

PRODIGY A cardinal alights in the uppermost branches above

my head, occupying this city of sky with its wild exclamation of colour ... the single longing note of its song.

PURITAN Most of all, I remember it as a time when ... *I could
dream.*

[THE PURITAN *moves off, lost in his own reverie. A burst of red
laser light surrounds* THE PRODIGY *in a cage.* THE PRODIGY *is
caught offguard and almost loses his balance*]

PRODIGY If I fell and broke myself on the ground I would lie
down there until morning. They would never think of
looking for me here. There is strange beauty in that.

[*Red lights shift. The eighth note from the ground bass sounds*]

VARIATION 8: PURE RECOGNITION

THE PERFECTIONIST *addresses the red light on his camera*

PERFECTIONIST Variation 8. Take One. There are moments in
life when one understands what it is one is really *doing*. For
an instant all the clutter is swept aside and the simple, obvious
fact of your being is captured in the mind's eye—a split-second
of pure recognition. I experienced one such moment early
on in my career on the occasion of a concert I did with Maestro
von Karajan. Now *there* was a transporting experience.

[*Music up: Beethoven's Third Piano Concerto.* THE
PERFECTIONIST *stands, moves away from the camera*]

You must understand that to me von Karajan was an Olym-
pian figure. Here was a living legend—a kind of God, really.
Night after night he stood at the centre of the world stage
and held Beethoven's beating heart in his bare hands. Von
Karajan on the podium while I played? It was beyond

dream. It was a new kind of wakefulness. Let's go backstage at the Konzertsaal ...

[THE PERFORMER *enters, charged up after a great performance*]

—our performance has come to a happy conclusion and I am floating on air! I wander the back corridors, hoping to bump into the Great Man. And there he is ... alone in his dressing room, savouring a glass of white wine ...

[THE PERFECTIONIST *picks up a glass of wine.* THE PERFORMER *is moving toward him now*]

[*as* VON KARAJAN] Mr. Gould. Come, come and join me. Tonight was—*superior.*

PERFORMER That's a great compliment, Maestro, thank you. I thought we acquitted ourselves rather well.

VON KARAJAN No, no, an *incomparable* delight. I thank *you.* It was one of those rare nights. The conductor, soloist, players, and audience, all of us soaring up and up and up! The world momentarily *one thing!* [*pause*] I *heard* you tonight, Mr. Gould. We all did.

PERFORMER And I could feel you listening. It was *electrifying.*

VON KARAJAN You must take that energy and give it to the world!

PERFORMER I'd love to but ... but I'm not entirely sure the world wants it, Maestro.

VON KARAJAN What do you mean?

PERFORMER The audience. Sometimes—not tonight, mind you!— but *sometimes* ... sometimes I think they resent me.

VON KARAJAN Of course. How is it possible not to have envy in the face of surpassing genius?

PERFORMER They stop listening and start watching. I feel it on my skin.

VON KARAJAN Some nights the audience will be a lover, another night it will be a wild, unbroken horse. It is a mental game.

You assume control by being in control. You will learn that there is much more to this business than the music itself.

PERFORMER I'm not sure I can accommodate myself to that.

VON KARAJAN I'm not talking about accommodation, Mr. Gould, I'm talking about *control.* For the audience you are a mysterious commodity. It is a game of mirrors. You must learn to play your image the same way you play your music.

PERFORMER But—

VON KARAJAN [*interrupting*] There is no other road for you to travel. You know, I heard Busoni, in 1924, just before he died …

PERFORMER Busoni …

VON KARAJAN … that was thirty-five years ago. I have heard no one better in the intervening years, until tonight …

PERFORMER *Busoni.*

[VON KARAJAN *pushes a vase holding a single rose into* THE PERFORMER*'s hands*]

VON KARAJAN Smell it, Mr. Gould. Let me see your smile. [*in* THE PERFECTIONIST*'s normal voice*] Extreme close-up. The split-second of pure recognition—

[THE PERFORMER *smells his rose and smiles. Lights shift. The ninth note from the ground bass sounds*]

VARIATION 9: THE ROAD TO MOSCOW

THE PERFORMER *is sitting on a suitcase, eyes glued to his wristwatch as he takes his pulse.* THE PURITAN *enters with a Brownie camera slung around his neck. He stalks* THE PERFORMER

SFX: Ethereal airport chimes. The opening notes of the ground bass

FEMALE VOICE [*off*] Le vol neuf-zéro-neuf d'Aeroflot à Moscou a été retardé. Veuillez écouter pour renseignements supplémentaires.

[THE PERFORMER *notices* THE PURITAN *for the first time. Gives his wrist a little rub as if he isn't really taking his own pulse*]

PERFORMER [*to* THE PURITAN] Did you happen to get that?
PURITAN Your flight to Moscow is delayed. I pray to God that doesn't mean you'll miss your concert.
PERFORMER Excuse me ... do I know you?
PURITAN You're Glenn Gould.
PERFORMER I am.

[THE PURITAN *offers his hand. They do 'the Gould Shake'— limp and tentative*]

Have a nice trip.

[THE PURITAN *doesn't budge*]

PURITAN I just flew in from Toronto. You were on the front page of the *Telly* yesterday.
PERFORMER [*pleased*] Is that so?
PURITAN [*seeing the headline*] 'Glenn Gould Soars to New Heights!'
PERFORMER My-my ...
PURITAN They went on and on about your concerts. From the sound of it the crowds have been going ape!
PERFORMER Overall, I'm very pleased with my performances. There have been moments of great emotional clarity. Thanks for saying hello.

[THE PERFORMER *opens a paperback book, sending what he thinks is a clear signal.* THE PURITAN *doesn't budge*]

PURITAN I'm sorry. It just gives me chills being around you.
PERFORMER Perhaps you're catching my cold. I haven't slept in

two days from the sinus pain. And now I'm waiting to fly into a spring blizzard in Moscow.

PURITAN You must be *terrified*.

PERFORMER This passes for normalcy when you're a touring concert pianist. One learns to put up with it.

[THE PERFORMER *goes back to his book.* THE PURITAN *holds his ground*]

PURITAN [*seeing the headline*] 'Plane Crash Claims Gould.'

PERFORMER I beg your pardon—

PURITAN [*eyes closed*] '... the crash occurred in a freak spring blizzard. According to eyewitnesses the plane skidded sideways off the runway and disintegrated in an enormous fireball. Already tributes from around the world have begun to—'

PERFORMER [*interrupting*] What are you talking about?

PURITAN I'm sorry, Mr. Gould, I have a vivid imagination, I got carried away. You're afraid of flying. I know all about that.

PERFORMER Well, we do our best. Nice talking to you—

PURITAN Funny, you're a man who fears flying but to me it seems like you live on the high trapeze! That mid-air moment, Mr. Gould! It's an honour to be in the presence of such bravery.

PERFORMER I assure you I am not a brave man.

PURITAN You're just being modest. If you weren't brave you would *never* get on this plane.

PERFORMER I'm the first classical musician from North America to be invited behind the Iron Curtain. It was a great honour to be asked. I could hardly—

PURITAN [*interrupting*] Ho-ho! I get the picture! You'd cancel but you *can't*—you're a cultural ambassador!

PERFORMER Radio Moscow has been playing my recording of the Goldbergs at all hours of the day. People lined up overnight for tickets.

PURITAN You're at the mercy of their insatiable demands!

PERFORMER I'm merely doing what I must do. My audience wants—

PURITAN [*interrupting*] Human sacrifice!

PERFORMER I'm afraid I don't understand the object of your enterprise here. I'm about to get on a plane and—

PURITAN [*interrupting*] I want to understand what makes you tick! Your bravery— [*raising his Brownie*] I want a picture of the way you think, Mr. Gould.

[*He takes a snapshot*]

PERFORMER [*flustered*] I am *not* a brave man! Do you want to know my terrible secret? Do you?

[THE PURITAN *backs off a step. Pre-recorded audience ambience comes up. Lights shift to favour* THE PERFECTIONIST *who sits in his swivel chair at the console. He draws* THE PURITAN's *attention away from* THE PERFORMER]

PERFECTIONIST It's a canon. We're supposed to be playing the game.

PURITAN I don't feel like it.

PERFECTIONIST It's a canon. You have no choice. If you were a household appliance?

PURITAN I'd be a vacuum cleaner.

PERFECTIONIST Hm. I immediately think 'information overload.'

PURITAN [*sardonic*] Think aluminum cylinder full of dirt.

[THE PERFECTIONIST *is grossed out, which pleases* THE PURITAN—*he returns his attention to* THE PERFORMER]

I don't mean to intrude, Mr. Gould. I find the power of your example ennobling. I simply need to understand—please—what *is* your secret?

PERFORMER Fish fly. Birds swim. I give concerts. Please—

PURITAN You're a phenomenon!

PERFORMER I'm merely a musician.

PURITAN But what a musician! You just told me people all over
the Soviet Union are glued to their radios!

PERFORMER That, sir, I can deal with. People sitting in the den
munching a perogi while they listen to Bach on the radio.
It's a hospitable image, scaled to the enterprise at hand—
which is, I believe ...

PURITAN Yes?

PERFORMER —the solitary contemplation of the beauty embedded in our musical literature.

PURITAN And fear never enters into it?

PERFORMER I have one great fear, and that is that events
beyond my control may divert me from my task. This flight
qualifies as one such event. As does this conversation.

PURITAN What if it never gets any easier?

PERFORMER Pardon?

PURITAN What if there is no end to the ... *difficulty?*

PERFORMER When total strangers walk up to me in public
presuming to know me—*that,* sir, I find difficult.

[*Ethereal airport chimes sound high overhead, notes from the
ground bass*]

FEMALE VOICE [*off*] Aeroflot vol neuf-zéro-neuf, un vol direct à
Moscou, débarque maintenant au gare vingt-cinq.

PERFORMER Zero hour.

[THE PERFORMER *stands up.* THE PURITAN *is suddenly overcome.
He so much wanted this to go well*]

PURITAN I'm sorry. I meant no harm, Mr. Gould. Your recording of the Goldberg Variations changed my life.

[*For an instant* THE PERFORMER *sees into this fan's vulnerability*]

PERFORMER I-I apologize for being abrupt. The last six months
have made me very aware of myself in the eyes of others.
The self-consciousness hasn't been useful.

[*SFX: A large audience before the lights go down.* THE PRODIGY *enters in overcoat and hat and stands to one side on the stage apron*]

PURITAN You were born to perform. Perhaps public scrutiny is a fact you'll have to learn to live with.

PERFORMER [*moving off*] There are no facts, my friend. We invent what we need and call it the truth.

PURITAN Godspeed—

[*SFX: Audience murmurs settle.* THE PERFORMER *exits*]

That fellow is amazing.

PERFECTIONIST You've forgotten how it *was* for him!

[*Lights shift. Another note from the ground bass. SFX: The sounds of an orchestra tuning up. The tenth note from the ground bass sounds*]

VARIATION 10: PELTED WITH ROSES

Single spotlight on the keyboard. THE PERFORMER *shuffles on-stage in ill-fitting evening wear.* THE PURITAN *and* THE PRODIGY *applaud along with a pre-recorded ovation.* THE PERFECTIONIST *watches, very uncomfortable with all of this*

THE PERFORMER *takes bashful bows. He's enjoying the ovation. This is* THE PERFORMER *fully in control of the moment, relishing his offbeat power.* THE PURITAN *and* THE PRODIGY *are right with him, wanting this to go well*

THE PERFECTIONIST *watches, biding his time*

THE PERFORMER *takes his seat at the keyboard*

Snap to black: We listen to Variation 10, early version

Lights up: THE PERFORMER *comes to his feet to acknowledge an enormous pre-recorded ovation which is echoed by* THE PRODIGY *and* THE PURITAN. THE PERFECTIONIST *bides his time—everything is right on schedule*

THE PRODIGY *gives* THE PERFORMER *a bouquet of roses.* THE PERFORMER *smells the rose as the crowd stomps and whistles and shouts bravos. He smiles and bows*

PERFECTIONIST [*to the audience*] Roses! He wants ROSES!

The audience throws roses which have been left on their seats with appropriate stage directions

THE PERFECTIONIST *springs into life—goes to his console to push buttons and tweak knobs. As the roses rain down the ovation shifts, sampling in strange new sound elements—the howling moan from 'the terraces' as a capacity football crowd in Northern Ireland pumps for the opening kick-off; eerie torch-lit chants from the Nuremberg Rally; the high-pitched ululation of Arab women from* Battle of Algiers—*we are caught in a maelstrom of unleashed aural emotion. All of it conducted by* THE PERFECTIONIST

THE PURITAN *reacts to all of this with alarm—his body language expressing physical pain*

THE PRODIGY *cheers on with a growing sense of alarm*

THE PERFORMER*'s bowing motion is contorted by the sheer weight of the audience's response as it continues to build into new levels of cacophony*

THE PERFECTIONIST *pushes more buttons. Lights shift to red. A sense of real danger now.* THE PERFORMER *is brought to his knees by the audience's response. He curls up in the fetal position as roses rain down upon him*

THE PURITAN *is frozen in a rictus of referred pain*

THE PRODIGY *reacts with shock to* THE PERFORMER*'s dilemma*

THE PERFECTIONIST *jockeys back his controls, pleased with the result*

Fade to black over this action, as the audience sounds diminish to rhythmic clapping, and finally to silence

The eleventh note from the ground bass sounds

VARIATION II: CHASING THE CADENCE

Music over: Sampled and looped fragments of the early version of Variation 11. Bach interpreted as polyrhythmic trance music

THE PURITAN *and* THE PERFORMER *remain on-stage*—THE PERFORMER *crumpled up in the fetal position,* THE PURITAN *in a rictus of referred pain*

THE PRODIGY *moves into the light, deeply disturbed.* THE PERFECTIONIST *appears, his eyes on* THE PRODIGY—*what is the kid going to do?* THE PRODIGY *helps* THE PERFORMER *to his feet.* THE PERFECTIONIST *goes to* THE PURITAN, *stands behind him to manipulate his arms.* THE PRODIGY *does likewise with* THE PERFORMER*'s arms*

Both THE PERFORMER *and* THE PURITAN *are in shock*

THE PERFECTIONIST *manipulates* THE PURITAN *to engage* THE PERFORMER *in a grappling match.* THE PRODIGY *moves* THE PERFORMER *so he can defend himself.* THE PURITAN *and* THE PERFORMER *grapple like Sumo wrestlers*

THE PERFECTIONIST *and* THE PERFORMER *name pharmaceuticals as they move, trading the brand names like insults*

Pharmaceutical list: Aldomet, Nembutal, Serpasil, Escadril, Chloromycetin, Stelazine, Largostil, Librax, Fiorinal, Inocid, Inderal, Zyloprim, Butazolidin, Bactra, Phenylbutazone, Methyldopa, Allopurinal, Valium

Uppers, downers, sleepers, relaxers—each drug has a physical effect on the opponent. A sense of 'emotional rollercoaster' here. Slowly but surely THE PERFECTIONIST *gets the upper hand, repeating the word 'Valium' over and over again to knock* THE PERFORMER *off balance and sap his energy*

THE PRODIGY *lets go of* THE PERFORMER. THE PERFECTIONIST *'rides'* THE PURITAN *off-stage, a literal monkey on the back, as he vanquishes* THE PERFORMER *with higher and higher doses of Valium*

Lights shift

THE PRODIGY *sits down at the keyboard. He has witnessed some unsettling events here which he does not understand. He needs to heal himself with music. He sounds the twelfth note from the ground bass*

VARIATION 12: THE VACUUM CLEANER

THE PRODIGY *practises the run up to a complicated cross-handed passage, stumbling at the same point each time*

THE PERFECTIONIST *comes back on-stage, catching his breath as he brings his full attention to* THE PRODIGY

THE PRODIGY *struggles with his fingering error, increasingly frustrated*

THE PERFECTIONIST *cues the technician. The red camera light comes on. He addresses it*

PERFECTIONIST I have a profound distrust of pianos. What draws me to Bach is the fact that the music *per se* transcends the whole issue of instrumentation.

[THE PERFORMER *wheels a vacuum cleaner on-stage, sneaking up on* THE PERFECTIONIST]

Bach shunned the outward disorder of musical appliances—

[THE PERFORMER *turns on the vacuum cleaner.* THE PERFECTIONIST *must shout over the noise*]

—and focused inwardly on the music itself, which he heard exactly as he wanted to! There was an incident in Tel Aviv which I think admirably—

[THE PRODIGY *stops playing and glares.* THE PERFECTIONIST *does likewise*]

PRODIGY Jessie! Can you turn that off? I'm trying to practise!
PERFORMER I have a different angle on the Tel Aviv story.
PERFECTIONIST It's a canon. You are to play the game.

[THE PERFECTIONIST *shuts off the vacuum cleaner*]

PRODIGY Thank you!
PERFECTIONIST If you were a bird which species would you be?

[THE PERFORMER *conducts himself, thinking.* THE PRODIGY *begins to play again, stumbling at the cross-handed passage*]

As I was saying—
PERFORMER [*interrupting*] A dodo, dodo. Excuse me—

[*He steps in front of* THE PERFECTIONIST *and turns on the vacuum cleaner*]

There was a peculiar episode in Tel Aviv which I think admirably demonstrates the point I'm trying to make about pianos.
PERFECTIONIST If you were a four-wheeled vehicle?

PERFORMER A Mack truck! I was on tour in Israel which, as everyone kept telling me, is a desert country and as a result seems to have bred a bizarre species of desert piano.

PRODIGY Jessie, I'm stuck on a problem! Finish the vacuuming later, okay?

PERFECTIONIST This will not do.

PERFORMER I found myself forced to give a series of concerts on a very bad instrument—

PERFECTIONIST —a monstrous pig of a piano!

PRODIGY I can't hear myself think! [*vacuuming continues*] Fine!

[THE PRODIGY *sings along with the music he's trying to play, to drown out the vacuum cleaner as he digs deeper into the difficult passage*]

PERFORMER This instrument had a terrible action, the equivalent of power steering, and it followed me along the rugged trail in its own special truck.

PERFECTIONIST There was no special truck! If you were a four-legged mammal?

[THE PERFORMER *thinks while he vacuums.* THE PERFECTIONIST *moves to regain control of the story*]

By the Tel Aviv engagement that piano was playing me!

[THE PRODIGY *races through the trouble spot again and again, singing the notes aloud.* THE PERFORMER *vacuums up* THE PERFECTIONIST*'s leg toward his crotch, horrifying him*]

PERFORMER An elephant in a zoo looking for peanuts.

[THE PERFECTIONIST *shuts off the vacuum cleaner.* THE PRODIGY *smiles and plays through the passage with ease*]

I took a long walk along the seashore and ruminated on my predicament.

PERFECTIONIST I *sat* on sand dunes! Play the game! If you were a machine in a science-fiction movie?

PERFORMER Hm ...

PRODIGY [*a major realization*] I short-circuited the problem!

PERFECTIONIST I decided the only thing that could save me was to re-create the most admirable tactile circumstances I knew of.

PERFORMER A teleporter! I literally transported myself to Lake Simcoe, sat down in our cottage at the old stubby-legged Chickering and *played* the whole concert through in my head!

PERFECTIONIST Right. Go on. We're all waiting.

PERFORMER Holding on desperately to the image of my performance at the Chickering I rushed to the auditorium, played the concert and for the first time on the entire tour I was absolutely *free* of commitment to that oinker of a piano!

PERFECTIONIST Aren't we marvellous?

PERFORMER And the Beethoven that came out was really rather extraordinary—

PERFECTIONIST —or at least you thought so. If you were a religion? [*to the audience*] It gets better. After the concert I'm in my dressing room and Max Brod—

PERFORMER [*interrupting*] —who is Franz Kafka's literary executor.

PERFECTIONIST A *religion*—comes back-stage with a woman who wants to meet me. She says—

PERFORMER Sufiism. She says: [*German accent*] 'Mr. Gould, I haf attended three of your concerts in Israel and tonight ... in some vay ...'

PERFECTIONIST [*German accent*] '—something vas different.'

PERFORMER [*German accent*] 'It was like your being vas not with us, you were ... *removed.*' Somehow she'd miraculously tapped into the mind-set I'd brought into the concert hall!

PERFECTIONIST Isn't that *lovely!*

PERFORMER Which made a pretty strong case for the existence of a privileged communication between live audience and performer!

PERFECTIONIST —a doctrine I find *highly* suspect—

PERFORMER —nevertheless, she'd put her finger *right on it.* I was spooked!

PERFECTIONIST Until she looked me straight in the eye and, in all seriousness, said: 'It vas unquestionably ze finest *Mozart* I haf ever heard!' Of course, I'd been playing *Beethoven!*

PRODIGY I can't hear myself think! Jessie! Turn the vacuum cleaner on!

[THE PERFECTIONIST *turns and gestures grandly. The stage is bathed in red light. The other players go into a freeze.* THE PERFECTIONIST *snaps his fingers. Lights up on the hanging piano. The thirteenth note from the ground bass sounds*]

VARIATION 13: BLOODSPORT

THE PERFECTIONIST *gestures to light and reveal the harp of a concert grand which hangs suspended high above the stage. He addresses himself to* THE PERFORMER *with quiet rage*

PERFECTIONIST Your problem, sir, is that you do not have normal filters for dealing with everyday situations and events. It can be dangerous out there if you're a peeled egg. The world bristles with sharp points and jagged corners. There came a time when you felt it all pushing in on you— it was the thirteenth of March ... the thirteenth of the third ... a very, very unlucky combination for you, my friend— your hotel room became ... a cage ...

[THE PERFECTIONIST *snaps his fingers.* THE PERFORMER *moves in a kind of waking dream to stand beneath the hanging piano.* THE PERFECTIONIST *snaps his fingers again,* THE PURITAN *and* THE PRODIGY *move to stand behind him. They too seem to be in an altered state.* THE PERFECTIONIST *gestures dramatically to*

the hanging piano, and it drops about a foot down toward THE
PERFORMER, *terrifying him*]

PERFORMER I-I call friends in distant cities in the middle of the
night seeking comfort—

PERFECTIONIST You became a notorious canceller. Your
manager ran out of excuses.

[THE PERFECTIONIST *gestures toward the piano. It drops
another foot toward* THE PERFORMER]

PERFORMER [*more fear*] I-I tell them about the very real diffi-
culties and dangers I face and they take that as evidence of
my instability—

PERFECTIONIST Friends talk to friends. The circle widens. Soon
there is gossip between total strangers.

[*Lights shift to highlight each speech by* THE PRODIGY *and* THE
PURITAN]

PRODIGY They'd throw me a ball and I'd turn like this and let
it bounce off my back.

PERFORMER I'm easily hurt!

PURITAN I'd arrive in some major centre in the United States
and find myself *unable* to play.

PERFORMER It's a question of nerves!

PERFECTIONIST The next thing you know you walk into an
orchestra rehearsal and the room falls silent ...

[*The hanging piano drops another foot*]

PERFORMER Whispering behind my back ...

PURITAN & PRODIGY [*sotto voce*] Drinks Poland water. Never
shakes hands. Superstitious. And the pills!

PERFORMER I need them to sleep!

PERFECTIONIST The audience just eats all of this up. They love
the controversy! You've become another freak in the brothel

of show business. Which is where our friends the critics take over ... [*commanding the hanging piano with gestures*] '... seldom has a more exquisite performance been heard, or a worse one witnessed. Gould's pygmy piano stool, his storm-tossed mane, his habit of collapse at the end of each solo line were all sheer show business—'

PERFORMER [*bravado*] 'His brave interpretation of the music, sheer genius.'

[THE PERFECTIONIST *drops the piano another foot.* THE PERFORMER *cowers*]

PURITAN All of this had a terrible effect on my playing.

PERFECTIONIST Columbia capitalized on the eccentricities from the outset, and early on you didn't mind the publicity ...

PRODIGY They were playing marbles in the schoolyard. I wanted to join in but the ground was so ...

PERFORMER I wear them because my hands are cold!

[*The threat from the hanging piano increases steadily. A sense that* THE PERFORMER *will be crushed at any moment*]

PERFECTIONIST 'It is a tragedy that Mr. Gould's behaviour at the keyboard produced laughter in the audience.'

PERFORMER I sing along because I can't help it!

PURITAN [*looking up at the dangerous piano*] Finally, the game got out of control.

PERFECTIONIST 'Why must he pounce upon the notes like a leopard upon its prey?'

PERFORMER My technique is self-taught!

PRODIGY Mr. Guerrero was inhibiting me!

PERFORMER No one understands!

PERFECTIONIST Mr. Gould seems to forget that he is on a concert platform!

[THE PERFORMER *comes to his knees*]

PERFORMER [*imploring*] No one listens!

PERFECTIONIST You, my friend, have a hearing problem!

[*SFX: Fish sting. The piano drops toward* THE PERFORMER. *Snap to black. The fourteenth note from the ground bass sounds*]

VARIATION 14: HE HURT ME

THE PERFECTIONIST *gestures to fly the piano harp back up into the hanging position.* THE PERFORMER *is splayed on the floor beneath it*

PERFECTIONIST I've always been a fanatic about pianos. My concern is not about the sound so much as the *action.*

[THE PERFORMER *raises himself on one elbow, groans.* THE PERFECTIONIST *is dismayed*]

PERFORMER [*checking the back of his head for blood*] October and November, 1959. Berkeley, Denver, San Francisco, Atlanta, Rock Hill, Cincinnati, Bloomington, Cleveland, Syracuse, Oklahoma City. A different bad piano every night. The world moving fast, the borders blurring.

[THE PERFORMER *comes unsteadily to his feet.* THE PERFECTIONIST *is irritated by his recovery*]

PERFECTIONIST For me it's all about the draft of the keys. Tactile grab and immediacy.

PERFORMER [*touching his chest*] I'd lost my home here ...

PERFECTIONIST This is 'tactile immediacy.' [*he plucks a string*]

[THE PERFORMER *clutches his chest*]

PERFORMER [*sitting on his piano chair*] At the end of the tour I had to fly to Manhattan for a meeting with the people at

Steinway about my recording schedule.

PERFECTIONIST With every keyboard instrument you're dealing with a time lag between pushing the key, and getting this ...

[THE PERFECTIONIST *plucks the string again.* THE PERFORMER *reacts. Overlapping begins.* THE PERFORMER *continues in his post-injury haze*]

PERFORMER Jan Hubbert was the chief technician at Steinway. A remarkable man in his own way—a piano tuner elevated to a position only slightly below [THE PERFECTIONIST *starts here*] the master musicians whose instruments he serviced.

PERFECTIONIST Bearings, levers and linkages. Every one of them requires time to complete its cycle ...

PERFORMER Hubbert and I had had increasingly sharp disagreements about the regulation of pianos, which we both repressed.

PERFECTIONIST No slack! Shallow draft on the keys, everything else cranked down two turns past tight. I want to feel the musculature of the music.

PERFORMER I wanted things done to my piano that Hubbert simply would not do—mechanical adjustments [THE PERFECTIONIST *starts here*] that he felt were out of bounds.

PERFECTIONIST Every note sharply etched in a discrete sound envelope.

PERFORMER So this antagonistic friction developed.

[THE PERFECTIONIST *glares at* THE PERFORMER]

PERFECTIONIST I don't want to think about the instrument that's between me and my mental image of the music.

[THE PERFECTIONIST *approaches* THE PERFORMER]

PERFORMER On the day in question Hubbert popped into my A&R man's office before he realized that Freeman and I were sitting there talking—

[*Enough is enough.* THE PERFECTIONIST *jumps in*]

PERFECTIONIST [*as* HUBBERT, *Dutch accent*] Hey, *Glenn!*

[HUBBERT *takes* THE PERFORMER*'s hand and shakes it heartily*]

PERFORMER Hubbert. I was just talking about you. You see I'm
planning to record the Tempest and we've got some new
ideas about the kind of preparation we'd like to try—
HUBBERT [*interrupting*] 'New ideas,' Mr. Gould?
PERFORMER [*momentarily flummoxed*] Yes.
HUBBERT [*big smile*] Here's hoping it doesn't involve tighten-
ing the action.
PERFORMER Well, as a matter of fact it does.
HUBBERT I'm afraid I've exhausted the possibilities of that little
experiment, Glenn. There's nothing out there but accidental
rebounds and hiccups.
PERFORMER Oh?
HUBBERT I'd have thought after the public response to the
Beethoven one-ten the desire for hair-trigger action would
have lost some of its allure for you.
PERFORMER I'm afraid I don't understand what you mean—
HUBBERT [*patting* THE PERFORMER *vigorously on the shoulders*]
Oh, you're a wily one, Mr. Gould. [*quoting review*] '… the
unnecessary clutter of unwanted sounds in the allegro
passages must surely be the consequence of a poorly pre-
pared piano …'

[*He gives* THE PERFORMER *a little shake by the neck*]

You do what you do best. I'll do what I do best. We'll get
along just fine.
PERFORMER He hurt me.

[*SFX: Fish sting.* THE PERFORMER *recoils in shock and pain.*
Lights shift]

It's the nightmare where you come to consciousness in a circus cage surrounded by sleeping tigers. You feel your way around the perimeter, looking for a way out before they awaken. Ears twitch and flick as you pass but their eyes remain closed. There is no door … no way out of the cage … and then you turn … and realize that one of the big cats is looking at you. It makes a little sound deep in its chest and rolls to its feet, the muscles in its back moving like slow pistons. You are out of control, in total freefall, but must pretend otherwise. That is the dominant feeling at the centre of this dream. You spot a whip and a chair in the centre of the stage. You move toward them as if you know what you are doing …

[*Lights shift*]

I said: 'He *hurt* me.'

PERFECTIONIST [*as a consoling friend*] The affidavit filed on my behalf in federal court charged that: [*reading the deposition*] 'Hubbert engaged in unduly strong handshakes and other demonstrative physical acts, ignoring the widespread and well-known fact that Mr. Gould was a man of extreme and unusual sensitivity to physical contact.'

[THE PERFORMER *is now sitting talking to a doctor who manipulates his left shoulder. Bending it into one uncomfortable position after another*]

PERFORMER Hold it like that?

PERFECTIONIST The initial injury was to the left side. When X-rayed—

PERFORMER My shoulder blade?

PERFECTIONIST … the shoulder blade was shown to have been pushed down about half an inch. This caused a very troubling secondary reaction; the nerve which controls the fourth and fifth fingers of my left hand had been compressed and inflamed.

PERFORMER My left hand ... when you move it like that ... ah!

PERFECTIONIST [*reading*] 'The defendant recklessly or negligently brought both forearms down with considerable force on the plaintiff's neck and left shoulder, driving the plaintiff's left elbow against the arm of the chair in which he was sitting.'

PERFORMER The doctor in Toronto gave me cortisone shots on alternating days ... no, it was worse than ever.

PERFECTIONIST I became so obsessed by this pain in my shoulder that Freeman had me seen by a friend at Johns Hopkins, a very fancy neurologist, and I insisted that he sit with me while I was being examined.

PERFORMER Anything ... a cast? Like this? Two months? Here? Alone? Yes. That sounds ideal.

PERFECTIONIST At the end of it all the neurologist took Freeman aside and said: 'Not a thing wrong with him.' [*laughs*] Nevertheless, as a result of this incident I was unable to play for six months and subsequently sued Steinway & Sons.

PERFORMER Steinway & Sons paid.

[*Lights fade. The fifteenth note from the ground bass sounds*]

VARIATION 15: THIS IS WHERE I GET OFF

SFX: Aircraft engines

Lights up on the four Glenns sitting in two rows of airline seats. THE PRODIGY *and* THE PERFORMER *sit together on one side of the aisle,* THE PERFECTIONIST *and* THE PURITAN *sit across from them.* THE PERFORMER *and* THE PURITAN *have the aisle seats.* THE PRODIGY *and* THE PERFECTIONIST *are at the windows. All are rigid with fear*

FEMALE FLIGHT ATTENDANT [*American accent. Off*] In preparation for landing please ensure that your seat belt is securely fastened and that your chair backs and tables are in the upright position. And thanks for flying American.

PERFECTIONIST [*to* THE PURITAN] The engine pitch changed.

PRODIGY [*to* THE PERFORMER] What was that bump?

PURITAN [*to* THE PERFECTIONIST] We're on our final approach.

PERFORMER [*to* THE PRODIGY] They put the wheels down.

[*SFX: Air pocket*]

ALL *Whoooooa!*

PERFECTIONIST [*whispering to* THE PURITAN] I have a terrible secret. I'm the only one keeping us aloft. Without me the rest of you disintegrate in an enormous fireball.

[THE PERFECTIONIST *pops open an air sickness bag.* THE PURITAN *leans across the aisle to* THE PERFORMER]

PURITAN Would you mind if we changed seats? I just realized I'm in 'E.' Not a good key for me.

PERFORMER My pleasure.

[THE PURITAN *and* THE PERFORMER *change seats.* THE PURITAN *is surprised and pleased to find himself sitting down beside* THE PRODIGY. THE PERFORMER *is less enthusiastic about his seat next to* THE PERFECTIONIST]

PURITAN [*to* THE PRODIGY] First flight alone?

PERFORMER [*to* THE PERFECTIONIST] You're looking rather bilious.

[THE PERFECTIONIST *puts away his air-sickness bag*]

PRODIGY Yes it is.

PERFECTIONIST Not you again—

PERFORMER We're joined at the hip.

PURITAN Afraid?

PERFECTIONIST That's a terrifying thought.

PRODIGY Terrified. You?

PERFORMER We have nothing to fear except fear itself.

PURITAN Speechless with anxiety.

PRODIGY What if we die?

PERFECTIONIST [*to* THE PURITAN] Humour him. He's only a child.

PURITAN We die a little bit every second we're alive.

[*SFX: Air pocket*]

ALL *Whooooa!*

[*All four Glenns take their pulses*]

PERFECTIONIST [*to the entire row*] Talk of death is surely premature. Might I suggest a simple exchange of pleasantries?

ALL [*to their seatmates*] Where you headed?

PERFECTIONIST This is my final trip to New York.

PRODIGY I'm giving up my piano lessons.

PERFORMER I'm abandoning the concert stage.

PURITAN I-I'm not sure where I'm headed.

PERFECTIONIST Perhaps if we played the game we could stabilize this situation— [*to the row*] Concentrate on flying! If-if you were a-a bird what species would you be?

PRODIGY I'd be a budgie—safe and happy and in the kitchen.

PERFORMER A peregrine falcon—soaring high above the Arctic wastes.

PERFECTIONIST [*to* THE PERFORMER] No! You're a bower bird—trapped in your ritualized display.

PURITAN [*indicating* THE PERFORMER] He already told you—a dodo—flightless, overly specialized.

PERFECTIONIST My good man, 'extinction' is officially off-limits!

[*SFX: Air pocket*]

ALL *Whoooaaa!*

PURITAN [*to* THE PRODIGY] Are those runway lights?
PERFORMER [*to* THE PERFECTIONIST] What was that bump?
PRODIGY [*to* THE PERFECTIONIST] The flaps.
PERFECTIONIST We'll be home before you know it.
ALL This is it!

[*Everyone tenses and leans back as the plane comes in for a landing*]

PRODIGY Tell mother I loved her!
PERFORMER A blinding flash of glory! *Perfect!*
PERFECTIONIST My conscience is clear!
PURITAN Not yet!

[*Snap to black. Music up: Excerpt from Bach's Fourth Partita. Lights shift. The mood of the travellers has settled*]

PRODIGY Bach's Fourth Partita. Some day I'll play like that.
PERFECTIONIST April 10, 1964, The Wiltshire Ebell Theater in Los Angeles.
PERFORMER My last public performance.
PERFECTIONIST [*to* THE PERFORMER] You bowed and I walked off the stage. Never to return.
PERFORMER The end of all applause.
PURITAN Surely one thing ends so another can begin.

[*SFX: Tires hit runway. The Glenns bounce once as the plane lands, then applaud the pilot's skill, joined by the sound of audience applause. Audience applause continues, under*]

ALL First Rate! Outstanding! Superb! Brilliant!

[*The applause continues as they come to their feet*]

PRODIGY [*to* THE PERFECTIONIST, *finally getting it*] Are you ... are you *Glenn Gould?* [*to* THE PERFORMER] Gould? Glenn Gould! The noted Canadian pianist. [*to* THE PURITAN] You're Gould, aren't you?

[*The four of them exchange eye contact*]

PURITAN, PERFORMER & PERFECTIONIST Glenn *Gould?* Never heard of him.

[*The four Glenns stand together and take bows*]

ALL This is where I get off.

[*They exit. Fade to black. The sixteenth note from the ground bass sounds*]

End of Act I

THE INTERVAL

VARIATION 16: THE FRENCH OVERTURE

The early version of Variation 16 carries the audience up the aisles and out of the performing area

During the half-hour 'Quiet in the Land,' 'The Idea of North' and 'The Latecomers' are played in the various lobby areas

The audience returns to the accompaniment of the late version of Variation 16

At the end of the Variation, lights fade. The seventeenth note from the ground bass sounds

ACT II

VARIATION 17: THE SOUND OF MYSELF

Lights up: Firelight flickers. THE PRODIGY *enters reading a book*

PRODIGY [*impressed by what he's just read*] Franzie-boy, you got it nailed! An artist must *remove* himself from the world! It's all right here! [*reading*] 'That is why one can never be alone enough when one writes, why there can never be enough silence when one writes. Why not even night is night enough.' Why not even *night* is night enough! Now, *this* guy knows how to have fun! I've got to get mother to read him! [*pause*] Sure thing ...

[THE PRODIGY *wanders to the keyboard. A minor chord sounds*]

I live in the key of F minor. Midway between complex and stable ...
[*another minor chord*]
... between upright and lascivious ...
[*an unresolved progression*]
... between grey and highly-tinted.
[*another minor chord*]
There is a certain ... obliqueness. A discordance ...
[*another unresolved progression. He stands*]
I release the trapeze bar ... I turn, mid-air ...
[*he hits a single note*]
I listen ...

[*pause, the note reverberates down to silence*]

I hear the click of a cell door closing.

[THE PRODIGY *closes the keyboard lid with a small click, goes back to his book*]

The world sleeps while I read my Kafka.

[*Lights up on* THE PURITAN *who reclines on a La-Z-Boy chair, opposite*]

PURITAN   No longer possible to play even a Bach chorale securely … parts were unbalanced, progression from note to note insecure …

[THE PRODIGY *moves again, coming closer to* THE PURITAN. *They remain unaware of one another*]

PRODIGY   Kafka smelled the rot in the world. [*looking at his hands*] If it weren't for this … I'd be a writer too. Roam the blank page with my perfect pitch, my sense of contrapuntal voicing. 'The Longing,' a novella by Glenn Gould, esquire. [*performing it*] 'He rose at dawn and—no—he *stayed up* until dawn and watched light come into the land in tinctures of grey. He knew it was going to be a long day, so many stations of the cross before he … before he … arrived—' Nah. Too slow …

PURITAN   … notes appeared to stick and scale-like passages were uneven and uncontrolled …

PRODIGY   [*recomposing*] 'He heard the longing call of a cicada across that August afternoon as he walked past the swinging porch chair where he'd spent so many lonely hours as a child.'

PURITAN   … an unpleasant experience, and seemingly immune to ad hoc pressures …

PRODIGY   I can see the reviews: 'The Longing' is a precocious first novel about a great pianist near the end of his days—a brave old man seeking refuge from life's last riddle. Is Glenn Gould projecting a future for himself here? Only time will tell …

[THE PRODIGY *paces, thinking*]

PURITAN ... wrist tightness problems ... separation into
bumpy groupings and a general lack of fluidity ...

PRODIGY Never mind that. Sunday painters read their reviews—
onward! Let me see: [*performing a line*] 'The great man
roams the endless night of the city, alone in his private
drama, a solitary traveller on a path that leads relentlessly
inward.'

PURITAN ... right wrist unbearably sore after any ten- or
fifteen-minute practice period ...

PRODIGY 'And now this call—his mother lies dying. He has
come down from the mountain to be at her side.'

PURITAN ... the fingers should not be required to move ...
only to 'be there' ...

PRODIGY 'The squeak of the stairs as he climbs toward her room.

[THE PRODIGY *moves around the piano*]

[*sotto voce*] So many things he must say to the dying woman.'

PURITAN Hear the blood in my brain ... the ringing ...

PRODIGY 'She sits in a reclining chair under a plaid wool
throw. She seems to be asleep, or perhaps not ...'

PURITAN ... nothing prevents the gradual deterioration of
image ...

PRODIGY '"Mother?"'

[THE PURITAN *sits up and rocks the La-Z-Boy into the upright
position. He has a cramp in his shoulder*]

She turns to look at him in the doorway. '"I am about to
die,"' she says, '"And that is as it should be. Why have you
come to see me?"'

[THE PURITAN *puts a thermometer in his mouth*]

The old man exercises his legendary control. All the words

must be in perfect order before he utters a syllable. He reaches into the glowing core of his being ...'

[THE PURITAN *comes to his feet wearily, heads off-stage*]

PURITAN I must write to the makers of Fiorinal— '... when combined with a certain state of hyperactive exhaustion your product delivers a superb waking nightmare.'

[*Lights shift. The eighteenth note from the ground bass sounds*]

VARIATION 18: ACTUALITY VS. REALISM

SFX: New York City street noise

THE PERFECTIONIST *strolls into the light, pondering over a yellow legal-length pad. He does not acknowledge* THE PURITAN *and* THE PRODIGY

PERFECTIONIST '—superb waking nightmare.' Laughter. Right speaker fades.

[THE PURITAN *moves into shadow*]

Left speaker—
PRODIGY I'm doing what I said I always wanted to do. Why can't she understand?
PERFECTIONIST [*circling a word on his pad*] Why *can't?* Why *won't?* Why *doesn't?* Wash from the Scherzo, and out.

[*Lights fade on* THE PRODIGY, *who, however, remains on the stage.* THE PERFECTIONIST *paces, looks up and down the street at the noisy traffic*]

Not *nearly* spontaneous enough—there's no sense of divine accident. And the central conundrum isn't clear—one should be half-full, the other half-empty—a dynamic equilibrium in the key of F Minor with *control* as the balance point.

[*Traffic noises up: honking horns, jackhammers, sirens*]

The driver from Columbia was supposed to be here twenty minutes ago. This is absurd ... taxi!

[*SFX: Louder street noise*. THE PERFECTIONIST *waves his arm as a taxi drives by*]

Five years since I quit performing you'd think I'd never have to travel against my will again. But nooo, that would be too easy. Every time I want to record I must make a nightmare pilgrimage to this ... this colossus that grinds human souls to powder. Taxi!

[THE PERFECTIONIST *waves his arm again. Watches another cab go by. Lights up on* THE PERFORMER *who sits in the La-Z-Boy chair under a plaid wool throw, jotting schematics on a yellow legal-length pad*]

PERFORMER The Central Conundrum: I give up public performance ... yet I still must perform for the public. [*writing*]
One is born with a gift ...
PERFECTIONIST These cabbies are driving by me as if I don't exist!
PERFORMER By early childhood the gift has overwhelmed all
else. [*a mother's voice*] 'Look what little Rusty can do at the
keyboard!' In the child's mind 'to be' is to perform.
PERFECTIONIST It's a kind of spiritual famine. Human hearts
for sale by the pound. One seeks perfection and is rewarded
with the experience of mob rule.
PERFORMER As he develops the Performer feels the walls
closing in—he is smothered by the expectations of others.
PERFECTIONIST [*looking around*] It sifts down on you all day
long in Manhattan. The spiritual soot of America. [*to
passerby*] I'm sorry, I don't carry spare change.

PERFORMER [*writing*] Emotion. Control. The moment of infinite privacy surrendered naked to the scrutiny of strangers.

PERFECTIONIST [*skirting a passerby*] Yes, that's a lovely ferret—I'm a skunk man, myself. Taxi!

PERFORMER Finally, he must withdraw from the world to exercise his legendary gift. He walks off the stage in Los Angeles and ends up in *this* chair at Uptergrove … lost in his own displacement.

PERFECTIONIST [*putting his yellow pad into a zippered attaché case*] It's no wonder I amuse myself with these autobiographical fictions.

PERFORMER [*writing*] In the story he tells himself 'I' becomes 'he' …

PERFECTIONIST It's a question of maintaining one's sanity.

PERFORMER The brain pressure is measured in tons per square inch.

[THE PERFECTIONIST *pops a pill*]

The deep question: What does the born performer *do* after he stops performing?

PERFECTIONIST Where is Theodore Slutz when I need him most?

PERFORMER [*in recognition*] He dons the disguise of the moment.

PERFECTIONIST Taxi!

[THE PERFORMER *gets up from the chair*]

PERFORMER Dressed as a guard … I walk backwards out of the prison.

[THE PERFORMER *puts on his 'Theodore Slutz hat'*]

[*as* THEODORE SLUTZ; *singing, New Jersey accent*] *The buildin's reach up to the sky / Traffic on the city streets / I sit alone and wonder / Who am I?*

PERFECTIONIST [*spotting* SLUTZ] Finally, this fellow seems to have noticed me. Now all I have to do is cross six lanes of rush-hour traffic.

[*SFX: Traffic noise up.* THE PERFECTIONIST *heads across the six lanes of traffic. It's a harrowing journey. He just makes it. Lights up to favour* THE PRODIGY *as he enters the action*]

PRODIGY New York City! This time next month I'll be there recording my first album. I've got to get mentally prepared ...

[THE PRODIGY *closes his eyes, does the 'taking flight' gesture*]

... imagine myself there in the best possible light. I swoop down on Central Park, the trees a nubbly lawn at my feet. Skyscrapers bend around the bowl of the sky. I bank steeply down Fifth Avenue ... come in for a landing at ... at Rockefeller Centre!

[THE PRODIGY *'lands' in Manhattan. Lights up on* THE PERFECTIONIST *and* SLUTZ *who are in a moving taxi-cab, in mid-conversation.* SLUTZ *talks into his rear-view mirror, adjusting it as he speaks with a 'rear-view mirror gesture' which will be quoted in later Variations*]

SLUTZ. [*New Jersey accent*] —and poof! there's a cloud of magic pixie dust and this teensy-weensy grand piano appears with a concert pianist yea-big standing beside it in white tie and tails. The guy at the bar turns to the genie and says: 'Hey, bubba! I didn't ask for a ten inch *pianist.*'

[SLUTZ *cracks up.* THE PERFECTIONIST *smiles thinly.* THE PRODIGY *is gawking at the skyscrapers*]

A ten inch pianist. It's, like, a word thing—
PERFECTIONIST Yes. I understand. Assonance.
SLUTZ [*rear-view mirror gesture*] Bet a million bucks you can't guess why I told you that one.
PERFECTIONIST Your reasoning, sir, is beyond me. The road, please.
SLUTZ Because you're Glenn Gould! I read your occasionals in *High Fidelity* magazine.

PERFECTIONIST My, my, a subscriber—watch out!

[*SFX: Squealing tires.* SLUTZ *swerves to miss* THE PRODIGY, *who is startled out of his reverie by the commotion. SFX: Street noise, traffic and pedestrians, continuing under*]

SLUTZ A survivor, Mr. Gould!

[THE PERFECTIONIST *is transfixed by the sight of* THE PRODIGY]

[*rear-view mirror gesture*] Theodore Slutz, taxi driver, avant garde musician—

PERFECTIONIST [*interrupting wearily*] —and music editor of 'The Village Grass is Greener.' Your reputation precedes you, Mr. Slutz.

SLUTZ That last piece you did about actuality and realism— very intense, Mr. Gould, very personal. *Very* personal, if you get what I get. I been thinking that—

PERFECTIONIST [*interrupting*] The distinction between actuality and realism is fundamental to the creative act in the modern era. And my train to Toronto leaves in less than ten minutes.

[THE PERFECTIONIST *can't take his eyes off* THE PRODIGY, *who rubbernecks at the tall buildings*]

SLUTZ I think the distinction is also fundamental to your private life, Mr. Gould.

PERFECTIONIST [*distracted by* THE PRODIGY] Sorry, I don't follow —maybe we should go cross-town and take Madison.

[*The cab moves forward in traffic.* THE PRODIGY *falls behind, pausing to check an address on a scrap of paper*]

SLUTZ [*driving*] If I understand you correctly, actuality is like the, uh, the rush of pure event unmediated by technology.

PERFECTIONIST You have an excellent memory.

SLUTZ Photographic, Mr. Gould. And realism ...

PERFECTIONIST Is the mind's photograph. An artificial event which can be infinitely manipulated by technology.

SLUTZ Which is where your personal life comes into it.

[THE PRODIGY *has caught up to them again.* THE PERFECTIONIST *is startled to see him*]

PERFECTIONIST I think not.

SLUTZ You're a born performer, Mr. Gould. The concert stage was your actuality and, like, now you've withdrawn into ... into this state of total realism. If you can dig that ...

PERFECTIONIST Never thought of it quite that way. You mean I've transcended my own chronology?

SLUTZ You've disappeared into your own rule book, Mr. Gould. I got a serious question for you.

PERFECTIONIST Shoot.

SLUTZ What happens to the Performer? Do you, like, keep that part of yourself chained to the dungeon wall, or what?

[THE PRODIGY *makes a direct approach to the taxi, aware of it for the first time*]

PRODIGY Taxi!

PERFECTIONIST [*panic*] My good man, I'm running rather late.

[THE PRODIGY *opens the cab door*]

PRODIGY I-I'm looking for Columbia Masterworks, two-oh-seven East Thirty Street.

SLUTZ Get in, kid. [*to* THE PERFECTIONIST] We can drop him on the way.

[THE PRODIGY *gets in*]

PRODIGY [*offering his hand to* THE PERFECTIONIST] I'm Glenn Gould.

[THE PERFECTIONIST *looks at the kid in horror*]

SLUTZ Check the gloves! Where you from kid, Greenland?

PRODIGY Toronto, actually. That's in Canada. Everybody up

there dresses like this in June.

PERFECTIONIST That's very funny. [*to the driver*] What is this? Some kind of free-form street theatre? Have you no respect for the boundaries of others?

SLUTZ All of this is, yunno, a ripple happening in my head— I'm doin' the changes on a riff.

PERFECTIONIST I have a very limited appetite for improvisation. Like your little game here, it's mostly cliché.

SLUTZ And you hate the Beatles! I don't get that, G.G. They're studio cats, just like you—

PERFECTIONIST [*to* THE PRODIGY] What are you staring at?

PRODIGY I'm afraid I-I've lost my direction.

SLUTZ [*rear-view mirror gesture*] Remember?

PERFECTIONIST [*to* THE PERFORMER] What are you playing at here?

SLUTZ Neither end nor beginning. Neither climax nor resolution. Like Baudelaire's lovers, the composition—

PERFECTIONIST Enough of this nonsense!

PRODIGY I-I thought I was imagining all of this.

SLUTZ [*singing*] *I sit at home and wonder / Who am I?*

PERFECTIONIST Utter gibberish! Stop this cab immediately!

SLUTZ Skippin' town, right? Never coming back here to record?

PERFECTIONIST That is the plan.

SLUTZ You're gonna set up some kind of basement recording studio.

PERFECTIONIST The Eaton Auditorium is hardly a basement.

PRODIGY I played my first—[concert there]!

PERFECTIONIST [*interrupting*] It's a handsome hall with a remarkably dry room tone. I can assure you *I* shall be very happy there.

SLUTZ Sorry, G.G. Bunker mentality.

PERFECTIONIST We shall see about that, my good man.

[THE PRODIGY *has picked up on the negative energy between his cab mates*]

PRODIGY [*to the driver*] This place is so different from everything I imagined.

SLUTZ Larger than life! [*rear-view mirror*] Right, G.G.?

PERFECTIONIST [*fed up*] Indeed. We apparently transcend the laws
of physics. My train leaves in eight minutes. Grand Central
Station is ten blocks from here. I'll do better on foot.

[THE PERFECTIONIST *climbs out of the taxi*]

SLUTZ [*after him*] Wash from the Scherzo and out, bubba!

PRODIGY I'm a little lost.

SLUTZ Relax, kid. Trust what you know. [*looking after* THE
PERFECTIONIST] And don't trust it when you know too
much. I'm afraid we haven't heard the last from that guy ...

PRODIGY I-I'm afraid I'm ... I'm a little confused. I was trying to
get mentally prepared to record my first album here and—

SLUTZ Beautiful, kid! That's really beautiful. Prepare to fall in love!

[*He flips* THE PRODIGY *an LP record. Lights shift. The nine-
teenth note from the ground bass sounds*]

VARIATION 19: ACTION AT A DISTANCE

THE PRODIGY *moves to the console, puts his album on a playback machine*

Music under: Variation 19, early version

THE PRODIGY *moves to the music, conducting himself*

THE PURITAN *sits in the La-Z-Boy chair doing hand exercises.
He is troubled by the experience. He reads from a yellow
legal-length pad*

PURITAN To Herbert von Karajan. From Glenn Gould, esquire.

Subject: Proposal for a collaborative recording. Dear Maestro: In response to your suggestion that we record together again I would like to make a modest proposal. As you know for some time now I have been exploring the technological and philosophical implications of the concept of 'Action at a Distance'—

[THE PURITAN *writes on his pad.* THE PERFORMER *schlumfs in, still wearing his Theodore Slutz hat, sits down in front of a television set, peels back the foil on a TV dinner, clicks on the set and starts to eat*]

PERFECTIONIST [*on the TV monitor*] Oh, I know what you're thinking. Here's old G.G. back to bend my ear with more tendentious twaddle about technology.

[THE PERFECTIONIST *on the monitor allows space for the others to speak. Nodding along with their thoughts*]

PURITAN [*reading from his pad*] I believe it is easier for people to show their better natures to one another if they are not in close physical proximity.

PERFECTIONIST [*on monitor*] Not a bit of it, my good man. You need know nothing of my theories about action at a distance to enjoy the output of my recording career.

PURITAN Technology makes this ideal possible.

[THE PURITAN *goes back to his writing.* THE PRODIGY *stops conducting and comes out of his reverie*]

PRODIGY I'm having a love affair. With the microphone!

[THE PRODIGY *waltzes with a microphone stand*]

PERFECTIONIST [*on monitor*] On the other hand, if you're interested in the psychological subsets—*why* Gould does as he does—let's just say I've taken certain home truths about technology deeply to heart—it might not be a bad idea to have a pad and pencil handy in case you want to take a few notes—

[THE PERFORMER *goes to fetch writing implements.* THE PERFECTIONIST *bides his time*]

PRODIGY It began years ago when I wandered into a living-room-sized studio and placed my services at the disposal of a single microphone belonging to the Canadian Broadcasting Corporation.

PURITAN Since I no longer travel by air it's been many years since we've met face to face. I regret this greatly.

PRODIGY I sat down and played two sonatas, one by Mozart, one by Hindemith, for live broadcast.

PURITAN I must admit a certain longing for another opportunity to record with you as I did in my youth. Thus this modest proposal for a rather unique collaboration between us on the Bach D Minor Concerto and the Beethoven Second.

[THE PRODIGY *conducts himself around the playing space, lost in the music*]

PRODIGY I communicated without being in the presence of a gallery of witnesses!

[THE PERFORMER *re-enters with a yellow pad and a pen, sits back down in front of the monitor, all ears.* THE PERFECTIONIST *smiles*]

PERFECTIONIST [*on monitor*] Proposition: Technology now mediates between man and the aesthetic experience.

PURITAN The creative parameters are as follows: Step One: G.G. and H.v.K. discuss, via telephone, all the relevant interpretive aspects of the scores—tempo, dynamic relation-ships and so on.

PERFECTIONIST [*on monitor*] Corollary: Properly applied, home playback technology can liberate the performer and equip him for a dynamic new relationship with both his audience and his music!

PURITAN Step Two: G.G. proceeds to pre-record piano parts, editing a two-track sub-master, which would be appropriately leadered, either for tracking or a mix, for stop cues during tuttis.

PERFECTIONIST [*on monitor*] Free of the obligation to grind out the same pound of hamburger night after night on the concert stage, the 'New Performer' roams at will through musical literature, the possibilities turn like shapes in a mobile as he plunges forward into new material, interprets it in the recording studio, then moves on to fresh challenges. At all points his view is panoramic!

PRODIGY [*producing a red acetate*] And *this* is my performance. An acetate pressing which captured all the felicities of the live broadcast. *This* is music that has streamed across the sky! Lightly, on the wings of the unchecked wind …

[*Music under: Excerpt from Moonlight Sonata.* THE PRODIGY *conducts himself with the 'taking flight' gesture*]

PERFECTIONIST [*on monitor*] The New Performer and his audience are wired into an enormous electromagnetic grid, they communicate synaptically, a global community of mind—

PRODIGY A single farmhouse with one light on. The rink out front where kids were skating. My music pours from the kitchen radio.

PERFECTIONIST [*on monitor*] It's an error to see these constructs as Orwellian, a technocratic conspiracy designed to strip man of his humanity. In my view technology exercises a kind of invisible charity.

PURITAN Step Three: H.v.K. would record the orchestral sections, using piano pre-tape.

PRODIGY The woman stops cooking, looks out the window into the darkening field … cocks her head … *listening* …

PERFECTIONIST [*on monitor*] The hierarchies of electromagnetic

radiation are the unheard harmonics of consciousness itself—
PRODIGY We intertwine like Baudelaire's lovers ...
PERFECTIONIST [*on monitor*] —and, in that respect, are on the
side of moral goodness and the sublime.
PURITAN Step Four: Where necessary we exchange footprints
i.e. orchestral material recorded first.
PRODIGY My music defying time and space!
PURITAN Thesis and resolution: That H.v.K. and G.G. can
have a meeting of the minds ... without the meeting.
PRODIGY A love-letter to the world ...

[*Music out*]

PERFECTIONIST [*on monitor*] I see this interactive electronic
complex as my playground ... and I look forward to having
you on the other end of the teeter-totter.

[THE PERFECTIONIST'*s broadcast ends.* THE PERFORMER *checks
out his notes.* THE PRODIGY *takes his record off the turntable*]

PRODIGY [*running off*] Mother! Look what I've made!
PURITAN The Maestro won't go for this, not in a million years.
He'll think I got off between floors. And if no conductor
will work with me on my own terms, then what? One must
press on toward the horizon, the thrust of living is its own
absolute ...

[*Lights shift. The twentieth note from the ground bass sounds*]

VARIATION 20: THE IDEAL PERFORMANCE

THE PERFECTIONIST *enters and moves to his swivel chair*

PERFECTIONIST I deeply resent the assumption that it is somehow fraudulent to splice together an ideal performance.

There are those who believe an artist's performance must
always be the result of some unbroken forward *thrust.* Some
sustained *animus.* Some *ecstatic high.* By my lights a worthy
performance reveals deep musical structure as a pure emotional line. If this 'ideal performance' can be better achieved
with illusion and fakery, I say more power to those who can
work that magic. The Tel Aviv Piano: Take Two! [*holding
up two pieces of mag tape*] A sand dune on the shore of the Red
Sea. Beethoven's Sonata No. 30, Opus one-o-nine. [*whisper*]
We hold the beating heart of the music in our bare hands—

[THE PERFECTIONIST *picks up a script, swivels in his chair and
gestures to alter the lighting for dramatic effect.* THE PERFORMER
enters, in a kind of daze. THE PRODIGY *moves to the piano.*
THE PERFECTIONIST *'conducts' their entries and exits throughout, following his script, mouthing key words*]

PERFORMER The *Red* Sea. Perfect. I've entered some kind of
demon world here. The compass needle spins in circles.

[*Music under. Beethoven's Sonata No. 30, Opus 109*]

PRODIGY I never listen to anything else when I'm preparing to
play Beethoven. Before Bach I listen to Strauss, Franck,
Sibelius, juke-boxes, anything. But nothing before
Beethoven. I must go in like a horse with blinders.

PERFORMER That stupid pig of a piano …

PRODIGY I always commit a new score to memory before I go
to the keyboard, to keep expressive manifestations divorced
from the tactilia. I don't want my fingers telling my brain
what to do.

PERFORMER I can't even remember what a real instrument *feels*
like.

[THE PERFORMER *starts doing hand exercises to limber up the
musculature of his fingers*]

PRODIGY There is a moment in Opus 109 which is a positive horror, and that is in the fifth Variation of the last movement. A moment which is an upward-bound diatonic run in sixths.

PERFORMER Not even a C Scale properly. I've got to *remember* ...

PRODIGY It's an awkward moment not only in terms of black-versus white-note fingerings but also in terms of that break in the keyboard around two octaves above middle C—precisely the point where Mr. Beethoven asks us to change from a pattern in sixths to a pattern in thirds. [THE PRODIGY *demonstrates the riff*] Sixths ... to this ... and you've got to do it in a split second.

PERFORMER —find the moment somewhere ... get inside it.

[THE PERFORMER *tenses in on himself*]

PRODIGY I had always heard this piece played by people who, when the moment of truth arrived, acted like horses in a burning barn—a look of absolute horror would come over them, and I always wondered what was so intimidating about it.

PERFECTIONIST [*cueing* THE PERFORMER] The deep emotional line!

[THE PERFORMER *does the 'taking flight' gesture*]

PERFORMER Uptergrove! The Chickering!

PRODIGY A week before the concert I decided it was time to sit down and play the piece through for the first time.

[THE PERFECTIONIST *conducts with building energy, vocalizing words and phrases when he can't control himself*]

Suicidal, [*with* THE PERFECTIONIST] but that's the way I always do things.

PERFORMER Light streams through the trees beyond the window ...

PERFECTIONIST [*cueing*] The lame can walk.

PERFORMER I move toward the keyboard ...

PRODIGY And the first thing I did, foolishly—very bad psychology—was to say: 'Well, let's try that tricky Variation, work out a little keyboard routine, [*with* THE PERFECTIONIST] just in case.'

PERFORMER Hold and refine the mental image ...

PRODIGY And as I began to work out my system one thing after another went wrong. Before many minutes had elapsed I'd developed a total mental block. [*with building anxiety*] I just froze at that particular moment.

PERFORMER Enter the time and space it occupies [*with* THE PERFECTIONIST] ... *be there* ...

PRODIGY I'm in the burning barn!

[THE PERFORMER *recoils in shock, this is not what he came for*]

PERFECTIONIST Stand by—

PRODIGY I've got to change the programme or delete the Variation or pretend that I know something about the score that nobody else does!

PERFORMER [*trying to convince* THE PRODIGY] ... the unheard music!

PERFECTIONIST [*preparing to cue*] Aaaaand—

PRODIGY [*overlapping* THE PERFECTIONIST] Then I tried the last resort method! I put a couple of radios on the piano and turned them up full blast!

PERFECTIONIST [*cueing*] GO!

[*SFX: Complex radio overlay. Chunks of strange languages hurtle by—BBC World Service. Radio Valpariso. A soccer game from Karachi. Snippets of martial music from the Soviet Bloc*]

PERFECTIONIST The charity of the machine!

[*Lights shift. The twenty-first note from the ground bass sounds*]

VARIATION 21: THE CANADIAN UNCONSCIOUS

SFX: Radio overlay shifts and continues, under

THE PRODIGY *listens at the keyboard.* THE PERFORMER*'s attention is on* THE PRODIGY

THE PERFECTIONIST *conducts the proceedings throughout, thoroughly in command*

The soundtrack clears, revealing the pre-recorded voices of the Glenns in close overlay

PURITAN ... when that first person heard that second person's voice by virtue of a crystal set, they had not only the most *unique* experience in music, of music in the sense of voice as sound but also that they had experienced [*cross-fade to* THE PERFORMER] *the only one true approach to radio.*

PERFORMER ... quite mysteriously, I discovered that I could concentrate more efficiently on a difficult piano score if I listened to two radios at once—the FM to hear music—

[*Cross-fade through difficult passage in Opus 109. Both* THE PERFORMER *and* THE PRODIGY *freeze whenever they hear the musical phrase. It's a little clearer each time we hear it*]

PURITAN That original human contact! That incredible, spine-tingling sense of awareness of another human being communicating something over great distance!

PERFECTIONIST I'm doing a radio documentary that examines the effects of solitude and isolation upon those who [*cross-fade to* THE PERFORMER] live in the Arctic ...

PERFORMER ... which I suppose demonstrates my inborn capacity to live contrapuntally. It was *precisely* this fascination with contrapuntal subjects which led me deeper into radio. I found that I could ...

[*Cross-fade through difficult passage of Opus 109. The fingering is more precise*]

PERFECTIONIST ... the people never actually meet ... the texture of the words themselves differentiate the characters and create dreamlike conjunctions within the documentary. [*cross-fade to* THE PERFORMER] The deep emotional line—

PERFORMER —counterpoint is not a dry academic exercise but rather a method of composition in which each individual voice leads a life of its own. It's the way our ears experience [*cross-fade to* THE PURITAN] the world—

PURITAN —in some subtle way the northern latitudes seem to have a modifying influence on our [THE PERFECTIONIST *starts*] national character.

PERFECTIONIST —a Russian doll approach to composition. Narrative nesting inside narrative in a documentary that thinks of itself as a drama.

[*Cross-fade through Opus 109. The passage is starting to flow*]

PURITAN —Webern-like continuity-in-crossover where motives which are resonant but not identical are used for the exchange of [*cross-fade to* THE PERFECTIONIST] instrumental ideas.

PERFECTIONIST The job will be to find concepts shared by all, then *draw* the characters into [*cross-fade to* THE PERFORMER] conversation about them.

PERFORMER Radio has always been of fundamental importance to Canadians and in that sense my current residency at the CBC is a kind of homecoming. Ours is a vast country, tenuously bound together by technology. I believe that—

[*Cross-fade through Opus 109. The difficult passage is perfectly transcribed.* THE PERFORMER *and* THE PRODIGY *are transfixed by the music.* THE PERFECTIONIST *hits a pause button*]

PERFECTIONIST [*live to camera*] —you get the picture, 'meaning' generates as a kind of unheard harmonic. When things work perfectly there's a sense that we're eavesdropping on a joyous whispering of secrets— [*to his engineer*] one more splice and we've got it nailed. [*he pushes another button*]

PURITAN To make a sweeping generalization, I think Canadians have a synoptic view of the world we live in. [*the tape begins to speed up and distort*] And in that regard I consider 'The Idea of North' a kind of national anthem, you know, [*strangely squelched*] chamber music for the Canadian unconscious ...

[*Fish sting.* THE PRODIGY *and* THE PERFORMER *go into a freeze. SFX: Thwacketa-thwacketa-thwacketa of broken mag tape*]

PERFECTIONIST [*cueing his engineer*] Stop tape!

[THE PERFECTIONIST *looks at* THE PRODIGY *and* THE PERFORMER. *Both are in physical disarray. He turns to smile at the camera*]

Don't worry, no cause for alarm. We leave nothing to chance here in Studio G, even the disasters are scripted. Unity. Cohesion. Structure. These are the things that matter most to us. I think we've made our point. It's all perfectible. There are no limits. Total control is the balance point. These beliefs we bind to us with hoops of steel ...

[*SFX: Telephone.* THE PERFECTIONIST *moves to the telephone, picks up. Lights shift. The twenty-second note from the ground bass sounds*]

VARIATION 22:
BEHAVIOUR & BELIEF / A FUGUE STATE

THE PERFECTIONIST *is on the phone, listening, rocking in his swivel chair, nodding, then saying 'uh-huh.' He repeats the sequence again and again*

THE PRODIGY *'plays' a modulated quote from Variation 22—a single musical phrase twisted into a seductive Moebius. The musical figure has caught* THE PRODIGY *in its thrall. He repeats it again and again, a stuck needle. As he repeats the musical phrase he repeats the series of physical moves involved in its playing*

For a moment we stay with THE PERFECTIONIST *and* THE PRODIGY *caught in their 'gestural loops'*

THE PURITAN *enters and repeats a pained hand gesture*

Light shift. THE PERFORMER *moves around* THE PRODIGY *at the piano.* THE PRODIGY, THE PERFECTIONIST *and* THE PURITAN *are unaware of* THE PERFORMER—*they continue inside their loops*

PERFORMER Concert hall audiences want that moment of ecstatic release … the most primitive human secrets worn on the performer's face. The French call it 'the little death.' I'll show you what I mean …

[THE PERFORMER *moves to a wheeled take-up bin with a roll of 35-mm film stock mounted on it. He checks film against his light.* THE PRODIGY*'s performance continues to build in intensity. Lights shift.* THE PERFECTIONIST *comes to life.* THE PURITAN *picks up a yellow pad and begins to make notes*]

PERFECTIONIST [*jovial*] … darling, it gets worse! [*reading letter*] 'When I heard you that night so long ago in Fort Worth'— remember now, this woman is talking about something that happened *nine years ago*—'I felt a rush of primitive carnal energy—' [*laughing*] I'm sorry, darling, I can't—*a rush of primitive carnal energy?* They're putting something in this woman's drinking water! I'm getting three of these letters a week! What am I to *do?*

[*He listens.* THE PRODIGY*'s performance continues to build.* THE PURITAN *writes on his pad*]

PERFORMER This is what I see: [*he 'reads' a sequence of frames*] The African veldt. Sere grasslands to the horizon. Acacia trees shift and shunt in the mirage while a pride of lions tugs loose the viscera of a standing wildebeest. Thirty feet of shining intestine.

[THE PERFORMER *is transfixed by the horror of his own description. For a moment the film stock becomes the intestine*]

PERFECTIONIST You don't understand, darling. I've never met this woman and she wants me to come and live on her cattle ranch in El Paso.

[*In the speech that follows* THE PRODIGY *becomes aware of* THE PERFORMER. *His playing of the phrase contorts with anxiety as he listens.* THE PURITAN *moves his attention to* THE PERFORMER *as well, feverishly making notes*]

PERFORMER The wildebeest stands splay-legged, motionless in the heat. There is nothing now but this. Head down, tongue lolling. The shock and ecstasy of public disembowelment.

[THE PURITAN *turns his attention to* THE PERFECTIONIST, *makes further notes*]

PERFECTIONIST Of course she's entitled to her feelings. But is that a licence to *consume* me?
PERFORMER He works hard to breathe, panting in hoarse gasps. He watches, wild-eyed, while the big cats settle to feed in

the wash of his living blood. This is what we came for. Catharsis ancient as the brain stem.

[THE PRODIGY *flees*]

PURITAN Wait!

[*Lights shift:* THE PURITAN *is at* THE PERFECTIONIST*'s console.* THE PERFECTIONIST *and* THE PERFORMER *go into a freeze.* THE PRODIGY *is gone.* THE PURITAN *comes forward to mount his yellow legal-length pad on a music stand. He gestures to bring down sacramental light on his offering*]

[*reading from his pad*] Catharsis, from the Greek *catharein,* meaning 'cleanse.' The warrior must be cleansed in battle. Before taking the field he must temper his sword with all that he knows, anneal the blade in the fires of his deepest beliefs.

[THE PURITAN *picks up his writing pad and moves toward the piano, reading from the pad. He speaks with great gentleness, an inward quality*]

I believe a musical performance is not a contest but a love affair and that love affairs must be conducted in private. I believe that public performance is the last blood sport and that applause is a shallow externalized expression of brute herd instinct: the howling mob is composed of passive individuals and passivity is the enemy of art. [*with growing conviction*] I believe that everything that is involved with virtuosity and exhibitionism on the platform is outward looking, or causes outward lookingness, and that that is sinful, to use an old-fashioned word. I believe that the purpose of art is the active lifelong construction of a state of wonder and serenity.

[*He moves past the other players one by one, addressing them individually.* THE PERFORMER *is first*]

Morality has never been on the side of the carnivore. Evolution is the biological rejection of inadequate moral systems. [*he turns his attention to* THE PERFECTIONIST] Our evolution in response to technology has been anti-carnivorous to the extent that, step by step, it has enabled us to operate at increasing distances from our animal responses. Technology imposes upon art a notion of morality which redefines the idea of art itself. [*he pauses, thinking*] The deep question is: *Why* do I believe as I do? Because my beliefs are true ... or because I need them for reasons that are forever lost in the rear-view mirror? The emotional line runs deeper still ... the warrior must see himself in a new light ... he must learn to *listen* ...

[THE PURITAN *gestures, changing* THE PERFECTIONIST *'s light.* THE PERFECTIONIST *comes out of his freeze*]

PERFECTIONIST What do you mean, darling? I brought this up because I think you're the closest person in the whole ... [*pause*] ... darling, please ... please don't cry ... I'm so sorry ... I should have ... I know, darling, I know.

[THE PURITAN *gestures to change* THE PERFORMER *'s light.* THE PERFORMER *moves to* THE PERFECTIONIST *'s swivel chair, sits down*]

PERFORMER [*'doing'* THE PERFECTIONIST] What I'm getting at here is that the experience of music should be closer to the experience of film. This Bergman movie, for example, the scene where Liv Ullman breaks down and cries? Watch it and you'll assume she emotes in real time. And you will be wrong. Less than ninety seconds of screen time, yet it took two full days to shoot.

PERFECTIONIST [*suddenly nervous*] Jessie just arrived, darling. I'm going to have to—I'll call you tomorrow. [*hangs up and turns, he tries to smile*] Well, Jessie, where have we been? [*the smile falters*] Yes, I am rather distressed. I was just talking to my dear, dear friend in Los Angeles. She brought it to my attention that it's two years since we broke off our relationship and I'm still calling her every day to compare intimacies.

PERFORMER Liv Ullman would be on a drip bag if she tried to sustain her emotional pitch for that length of time.

PURITAN [*dimming* THE PERFORMER's *light*] He doesn't know where he's going.

PERFECTIONIST [*to Jessie*] She accuses me of emotional manipulation. I must admit to a certain amount of confusion about her charges at the present moment. One sees oneself in a new light ...

PURITAN [*dimming* THE PERFECTIONIST's *light*] He doesn't know where he's been.

PERFECTIONIST [*to Jessie*] If I really love her I'm supposed to let her go and pretend there's nothing between us. I'm sorry ... I can't do that just now ...

[THE PERFECTIONIST *turns away from Jessie while he regains himself*]

PURITAN Technology allows man to experience the ineffable quality that art shares with prophecy—

[THE PURITAN *puts his yellow pad back on the music stand, gestures up to the lighting grid to sharpen the light on it. Then he turns to* THE PERFECTIONIST, *changing his light with another gesture.* THE PERFECTIONIST *turns back to Jessie. He's still distraught*]

—the capacity to serve as a mirror to those individuals who encounter it singularly.

[THE PURITAN *moves to stand directly behind*
THE PERFECTIONIST]

PERFECTIONIST Sometimes I catch a fleeting glimpse of myself, Jessie. My eyes in the rear-view mirror as I drive the streets of this city at three A.M., music at grand volume on the tape deck. I'm not going anywhere in particular, I'm just moving from here to there and back again ... a solitary figure in a landscape of sound ...

[*Lights fade on* THE PURITAN. *The twenty-third note from the ground bass sounds.* THE PURITAN *exits*]

VARIATION 23:
CONDUCTING THE SELF / SELF-CONDUCT

SFX: Telephone ring

THE PURITAN *enters talking on one telephone while he reads a newspaper. The other telephone continues to ring*

PURITAN —exactly the point I'm trying to make, Susan. You haven't *seen* me, but you *know* me. I mean, over the years we've spent literally hundreds of hours communicating telephonically, correct? Ah-ha. Ah-ha.

[*He cups the receiver, addresses Jessie's chair*]

Jessie, my private line in the study, could you take a message? Except if it's that fellow from Juilliard— [*into phone*] Sorry Susan, I've been rambling on here—the point I'm trying to make is that one can lead a solitary life without cutting oneself off from the world—mm-hm ... mm-hm.

[THE PRODIGY *enters holding a black telephone receiver to his ear. SFX: Telephone stops ringing*]

PRODIGY Jessie, sorry to call so early. Solitude makes one strangely convivial. It's like eating a pomegranate alone, one longs to turn to one's neighbour and compare notes. Listen, I was—what do you mean?

PURITAN [*on phone*] Mm-hm, to be seen by 'the other'—it's a
kind of emotional sustenance. Of course I've been thinking
about this a lot lately. I'm about to mount the podium and
try my hand at conducting a whole roomful of 'others.' I'm
a little topsy-turvy about how I'll be seen.

PRODIGY [*on phone to Jessie*] I've inverted my sleep cycle. I go
to bed at dawn, wake up when the light is beautiful between
the trees. For the first time I feel like I'm in control!

PURITAN Von Karajan once told me: You assume control by
being in control. Oh that it were so simple! [*laughs*]

PRODIGY Never mind all that, I want to tell you about this new
way I'm seeing myself! [*laughs*] Yes, Jessie, you have permission to unplug your tea kettle. I'll count to three—

PURITAN I think I may have reached an age where I know too
much, Susan, and that can be a dangerous state! [*laughs*]

PRODIGY —this state I'm talking about, this way of seeing
myself, it-it's hard to describe—it's like I suddenly realize
how much I already know—I mean, I know more than I
know, right? I haven't even unpacked the carton I came in
yet! Which has a lot to do with the way I conduct myself in
public—I have no idea how others see me!

PURITAN I'll be conducting in private, Susan. The Hamilton
Symphony. It's an experiment—

PRODIGY *Exactly!* It's knowing *what to do* with what you know
—which gets me back to this new way I'm seeing myself—

PURITAN Believe it or not, I've got a plan to conduct myself at
the piano— [*laughs*]

PRODIGY I was playing the Rondo from Beethoven's Concerto
Number One on the Chickering—fish-tailing through it at
breakneck speed. Instead of [*normal fast*] *dah-deetle-deet-dee
dah-deetle-dee-dee* [*etc.*]

PURITAN [*laughing*] Suppose it's Beethoven's Concerto
Number One. I'd conduct the orchestra to the piano
entry from my stool then— [*normal fast, with* THE PRODIGY]

dah-deetle-deet-dee dah-deetle-deet-dee— [*etc.*]

PRODIGY —it was [*breakneck speed*] *dahdeetledeedee dahdeetledeedee dahdeetledahdeetledahdumdumdumdum DUM!* It started to come in such a rush that I stepped outside the playing ... uh-huh ... *exactly* ...

PURITAN Right! And then I go back to my conducting—two-two-two Glenn Gould's in one! [*laughs*]

PRODIGY [*laughing*] I was hearing *all* the harmonics! I can't explain it, Jessie. The focus pulled way, way back. I was looking at myself across a great distance. I was ... a figure in a landscape. I'm a person who makes sounds, Jessie. And by making sounds I show people how I hear. Isn't that a strange thing to do with your life? [*pause*] No, I'll wait. Pour your tea. I'll go back to planning my novel.

[THE PRODIGY *picks up a yellow legal-length pad, begins to write*]

PURITAN Susan, I love talking to you but I've got to go. My cousin Jessie is here. Right, mm-hm. [*he hangs up, speaks to Jessie*] Juilliard? Drat. They think they have a volunteer for that little recording experiment I told you about. Hm?

[THE PURITAN *smiles, listening to Jessie. His smile fades slowly*]

Jessie, I'm sorry. I've given it due consideration and I am not, repeat *not*, interested in celebrating my fiftieth birthday.

PRODIGY [*reading his notes*] Chapter Two. As he nears his fiftieth year the ageing virtuoso decides it's time to pass the torch to the next generation. He arranges for a young prodigy to come and record with him, promising the lad he'll teach him everything he knows about playing the piano in half an hour.

PURITAN Jessie, it's not a question of health. I feel fine! I simply refuse to be trapped by that kind of chronology. The calendar is a tyrant. Once you submit to its relentless linearity you're ... *you're* finished. No party, understand? Go. Call my father. Tell him.

PRODIGY The lad's name is ... Steven Prince, no, too direct,

Steven *Price*—the most promising student at Juilliard. With his heart in his throat the boy telephones the great man to make the necessary arrangements—

[*SFX: Telephone rings.* THE PURITAN *picks up*]

PURITAN Ah, Steven Price—I've been waiting for your call. I'm thrilled that you've agreed to go along with my little experiment! Now, as to dates—

PRODIGY When the old man answers the boy is awestruck. He can hear himself babbling.

[THE PRODIGY *makes more notes. His pen is running out of ink*]

PURITAN Pardon me? The twenty-seventh? No, that's a very, very unlucky number for me, Steven. I would never have anyone I knew flying on the twenty-seventh. How about the twenty-eighth? Uh-huh. Uh-huh.

PRODIGY At a critical moment the lad's pen runs dry. He uses the blunt tip to emboss the date of their meeting on a scratch pad. He mumbles words of homage ...

PURITAN Nonsense, Steven, you're helping *me* fulfill a lifelong dream to conduct. I'll make this promise to you—come to Toronto and I'll teach you everything you need to know about playing the piano in half an hour. The twenty-eighth, Steven. I'll have my people send you a ticket.

[THE PURITAN *hangs up the phone, thinks, smiles, writes on his pad.* THE PRODIGY *writes on his pad. The lights fade on them*]

PRODIGY Jessie, you're back—listen, the thoughts are coming so fast right now. What I'm trying to say is I really think there's a way I can *live.* I'm starting to see myself in the future, and I like what I see ... I'm growing up, Jessie. I'm finally learning how to conduct myself ...

[*Lights fade. The twenty-fourth note from the ground bass sounds*]

VARIATION 24: THE CENTIPEDE

Lights shift to favour THE PRODIGY. *He begins to conduct*

THE PERFECTIONIST *moves into the light and begins quoting from the compendium of gestures developed thus far.* THE PRODIGY *cues the entrance of* THE PERFORMER *and* THE PURITAN—*they, too, quote from the gestural vocabulary. A sense of centipedal motion between the three of them*

At THE PRODIGY's *command* THE PERFECTIONIST *starts singing, the others join in one by one, turning the song into a round*

PERFECTIONIST [*tenor, repeating*] *Grey light, grey land / The mind-body problem.*
PERFORMER [*alto, repeating*] *I live in this moment / Let me live in this moment!*
PURITAN [*bass, repeating*] *I want to be alone / I'll call you every night.*

[THE PRODIGY *speeds up the tempo. A feeling of 'Sorcerer's Apprentice' to all this.* THE PRODIGY *is unleashing forces beyond his command*]

PERFECTIONIST *Grey light, grey land / The mind-body problem.*
PERFORMER *I live in this moment / Let me live in this moment!*
PURITAN *I want to be alone / I'll call you every night.*

[*SFX: Sound Cluster #1: a raging fire. Lighting effects eat hungrily around the walls of the theatre. Sirens whoop and wail. A police radio crackles: 'We got a three alarm at the Eaton auditorium on College.'* THE PERFECTIONIST *falls out of the centipede and watches the dancing flames in horror*]

PERFECTIONIST [*tenor, repeating*] I *want to be alone / I'll call you every night.*
PERFORMER [*alto, repeating*] *Grey light, grey land / The mind-body problem.*

PURITAN [*bass, repeating*] *I live in this moment / Let me live in this moment!*

[*SFX: Sound Cluster #2: We hear the beep-beep-beep of a life - support system. The voice of a doctor: 'The family has asked us to disconnect all life support.'* THE PURITAN *looks on, horrified, and falls out of the centipede.* THE PRODIGY *tries to conduct the flow of events without success. The situation is out of control*]

PERFECTIONIST [*alto, repeating*] *I live in this moment / Help me live in this moment!*

PERFORMER [*tenor, repeating*] *I want to be alone / I'll call you every night.*

PURITAN [*bass, repeating*] *Grey light, grey land / The mind-body problem.*

[*SFX: Sound Cluster #3: Workmen shout harried instructions as they lose control of a crated grand piano: 'Take it easy, this is Gould's piano. Watch it! WATCH IT!'* THE PRODIGY *moves to protect* THE PERFORMER *as the hanging harp of a grand piano falls toward him. Snap to black. The twenty-fifth note from the ground bass sounds*]

VARIATION 25: LOSS

Lights up on a series of images

Music up: Variation 25, late version

Playing area #1: The music stand. THE PURITAN *presides, writing on his yellow legal-length pad*

Playing area #2: A hospital bed. THE PERFECTIONIST *in residence, propped up facing the audience*

Playing area #3: THE PERFORMER *down on one knee, a tableau of grief*

In shadow: THE PRODIGY *sways with the emotional contours of Variation 25. He moves into the light*

PRODIGY I was playing the piano beside the picture window this afternoon. A cardinal flew headlong against the glass not six inches from my face ...

[*SFX: Fish sting.* THE PERFORMER *reacts*]

PERFECTIONIST [*addressing* THE PERFORMER] She never understood, Jessie.

PRODIGY ... its body landed in the snow. I sat there and waited for the bird to recover.

[THE PRODIGY *sits on the piano chair*]

PERFECTIONIST She'd read something in the newspaper and go straight to the telephone. [*doing mother's voice*] Glenn, it says here that you make your employees take an oath of secrecy—is that true? What are you trying to hide? And what's this about stuffing yourself with doughnuts in the middle of the night? Why aren't you eating properly?

[THE PERFECTIONIST *struggles to control his emotions.* THE PERFORMER *is fully aware of* THE PERFECTIONIST]

It's all very funny, really. This loss ...

[THE PERFORMER *comes to his feet with difficulty*]

PURITAN [*stopping to read from his pad*] Dizziness ... right arm numb ... palpitations ... short of breath ... a ringing in the ears ...

[THE PRODIGY *waits for the cardinal to recover.* THE PERFORMER *is now at the foot of* THE PERFECTIONIST*'s bed*]

PERFECTIONIST I'd say to her: Mother this recluse business is all part of the publicity game. She didn't want to believe that. Why are you always getting sick, she'd say. Is that part

of the publicity game too? She never understood the reality
of my condition. What was I supposed to do? Dismantle my
body in front of her like a broken toaster?

PURITAN [*reading*] I returned to a whole-body system, employ-
ing hand-knuckle-bridge, high wrist monitor and constant
adjustment to back.

[THE PERFORMER *moves to take up Jessie's eyeline with* THE
PERFECTIONIST]

PERFECTIONIST [*to* THE PERFORMER] Jessie, listen to me. I have
symptoms! When I stand up my legs are numb! And the dizziness
—labyrinthisis is a very real disorder caused by a viral infection
in the inner ear. I've had it for years and there's no known cure!
This is *illness*, Jessie, not behavioural disorganization!

PURITAN [*reading his notes*] During mid-summer much effort was
directed to the hand-knuckle and initially it appeared that some
progress was made when these were subject to indent pressure.
This seemed to foster crescent-like sensations in the hands
which offered a partial solution.

[THE PRODIGY *experiences 'crescent-like sensations' in his hands.
He realizes that the cardinal is not going to recover*]

PRODIGY All of it ... *borrowed.*

PERFECTIONIST The hot wax, could you?

[THE PERFORMER *picks up an aluminum basin of hot wax.
Takes it to* THE PERFECTIONIST *who dips his hands*]

PURITAN [*writing*] In late summer conducted experiments with
elevated wrists. These inaugurated to alleviate unnatural
burden in indented fingers, thumbs and knuckles. The
experiment resulted in complete loss of control.

[THE PERFECTIONIST *flexes his hands, breaking the wax sheath.*
THE PRODIGY *stands*]

PRODIGY Two full minutes. No movement. Just the wind in its breast feathers.

PERFECTIONIST [*laughing to himself*] Remember how she made me see red? I recall once being so angry that I wanted to kill her. I can assure you there are few people in this world who have aroused those passions in me.

PRODIGY I went out into the snow in my stocking feet. Four o'clock, a February afternoon in Ontario. That beautiful light through the trees.

[THE PRODIGY *bends in a slow gesture of grief*]

PURITAN [*'narrating'* THE PRODIGY's *move*] Tried holding wrist tightly from beneath so as to use it as fulcrum-like constant. At the same time tipping the head towards right shoulder and moving it as a unit so the fingers would be there when needed.

PRODIGY I picked up the broken bird, such a wild exclamation of colour—

PURITAN One day wonder.

PRODIGY —carried him back inside. I've been playing the twenty-fifth Variation over and over again ever since ... fitting it to the mood of the moment ... the wistful and weary core of this day ...

PURITAN [*reading*] No longer possible to play even Bach chorale securely.

PRODIGY ... slowing it down ... relaxing the moments between the notes.

PURITAN Parts were unbalanced, progression from note to note insecure.

PRODIGY ... opening a space for his final flight.

PURITAN Nothing prevented the gradual deterioration of image.

PRODIGY There's no such thing as 'going too slow' in a moment like that.

PERFECTIONIST She was in the dream I had last night, Jessie. She was sitting in the window chair at Uptergrove watching a bird at the feeder. Hands crossed like this ... silent while she watched me enter the room. 'I am about to die and that is as it should be,' she said, 'Why have you come to see me?'

[THE PERFECTIONIST *extends his hand to* THE PERFORMER. THE PERFORMER *moves to comfort* THE PERFECTIONIST. *It is an act of compassion and surrender*]

I believe in the hereafter, Jessie. I believe that all the spiritual energy that has ever been is with us now, radiant and invisible. We should not confuse ourselves with these bodies. I am not this body. I am an electromagnetic field that *animates* this body. Did you know that every single atom on the earth has been through *three* supernovae cycles? We're made out of atoms that were created inside exploding stars! Think of it, Jessie. [*looking at his hands*] Billions upon billions of years old.

[*Lights fade on* THE PERFECTIONIST. *He lies down and pulls the covers over his head*]

PRODIGY The cardinal is on the kitchen table in a Birks box. When dawn comes up I'm going to bury him like an Egyptian pharoah. In the meantime, there is a grace note in this silence. The tone of the experience without the experience itself. I stand in the nave of Bach's cathedral. I listen.

[*SFX: The moan of Arctic wind. Lights fade. The twenty-sixth note from the ground bass sounds*]

VARIATION 26: THE PSYCHOLOGICAL SUB-TEXT

Lights shift

THE PERFECTIONIST *remains alone in his hospital bed.* THE PURITAN *makes a vaudeville entrance da-daing his way through*

'Be kind to your fine feathered friends / That duck may be somebody's brother.' *He marches around* THE PERFECTIONIST *'s bed, doing his best to cheer up the sick room*

PURITAN Good evening, and welcome to another edition of 'Brain Peelers'! My name is S.F. Lemming and my guest this evening is Dr. Wolfgang von Krankmeister, the editor of 'Insight,' the Journal of the North Dakota Psychiatric Association. Our subject this evening, that kooky Canadian virtuoso, Glenn Gould! [*cueing theatrically*] TA-DA!

[*SFX: Arctic wind. The television monitor shows a vista of Arctic landscape.* THE PERFORMER *comes on-screen, broadcasting from a live camera off-stage. He has binoculars slung around his neck. He leans into the wind, holds the binoculars to his ear, checking the horizon.* THE PERFECTIONIST *is amused, despite himself. He can't resist playing into* THE PURITAN *'s gambit, if grudgingly*]

PERFECTIONIST [*German accent*] Vat a pity. I come prepared to talk about Franz Kafka.

[*The Arctic wind stops, replaced by violin schmaltz from a Prague café, circa 1920*]

PURITAN Kafka is next week, Dr. von Krankmeister. This is the twenty-sixth.

[*The Arctic wind comes back*]

PERFECTIONIST Oh vell, ve do da cut and paste, yah?

[*The Arctic wind and the Prague violin music commingle and continue throughout, under*]

PURITAN What we're trying to understand here are the career choices Glenn Gould made as a performer.
PERFECTIONIST Da psychological sub-text—

PURITAN Precisely … could we roll footage?

[THE PURITAN *cues* THE PERFORMER. THE PERFORMER *plays out his dialogue with an ironic edge, he's delivering* THE PERFECTIONIST*'s words back to him*]

PERFORMER [*on monitor*] Proposition: Solitude is the prerequisite for ecstatic experience and the condition of heroism. As the concert stage recedes in memory I find more and more that I separate myself from conflicting and contrasting notions. Monastic seclusion works for me.

[THE PERFORMER, *on monitor, holds his binoculars to his ear and scans the horizon*]

PERFECTIONIST Da typical schizoid dilemma! Desperate need for luf combines vis da equally desperate fear of da close involvement. Vhen Kafka enters his private prison in Prague he—
PURITAN [*interrupting*] We're talking about Glenn Gould.

[THE PURITAN *begins a tug of war, trying to pull* THE PERFECTIONIST *into an upright position*]

PERFECTIONIST [*resisting him*] Da size of an unknown object can't be measured vithout another object of known size as reference! Kafka, ve know! Mister Schtick-in-da-Mud!

[THE PURITAN *succeeds in getting* THE PERFECTIONIST *into a sitting position*]

PERFECTIONIST Gould vas more … more vhat? More slippery.

[THE PERFECTIONIST *slithers back under the covers.* THE PURITAN *blocks him. They play out more vaudeville tug-of-war business*]

PURITAN I would maintain that Gould neutralized his neurosis by turning it into a vaudeville.
PERFECTIONIST But vas he ever really *free?*

[THE PERFECTIONIST *cues* THE PERFORMER]

PERFORMER [*on monitor*] I would like to try my hand at being a prisoner, on the understanding, of course, that I would be entirely innocent of all charges brought against me.

PERFECTIONIST —an innocent prisoner. Just like poor Franz.

[THE PERFECTIONIST *dives back under the covers.* THE PURITAN *tries to secure an arm or a leg*]

PURITAN Forget Kafka. I want to get at the root of Gould's bravery.

[THE PURITAN *cues* THE PERFORMER, *pulls* THE PERFECTIONIST *out of bed by the legs.* THE PERFECTIONIST *struggles heroically*]

PERFORMER [*on monitor*] One can't feel oneself heroic without having first been cast off by the world, or better still, by having done the casting off oneself.

[THE PERFECTIONIST *is on his back on the floor now*]

PERFECTIONIST Vat's your point?

PURITAN Proust said: 'Everything great comes from neurotics. They alone have founded religions and produced our masterpieces.'

[THE PURITAN *tries to pull* THE PERFECTIONIST *to his feet*]

PERFECTIONIST Patent nonsense. [*slithering under the bed*] Franz retreats from da verlt zo to obey laws of his own personality vich in da 'normal context' threaten to tear him apart!

[THE PURITAN *pulls* THE PERFECTIONIST *from under the bed. Hauls him to his feet*]

PURITAN Your point, I suppose, is that Gould and Kafka are aspects of the same Jungian type—

[THE PURITAN *starts walking him around*]

PERFECTIONIST Dey vas joined at da hip!

[*They circle the bed together*]

PURITAN I totally disagree. Gould's gift was an act of extreme extroversion—he had an overpowering need to dramatize his dilemma. Witness his invention of you, Herr von Krankmeister. Kafka, on the other hand, was an extreme introvert.

PERFECTIONIST Behavioural disorganization and neurosis follows vhen introversion or extroversion gets out of vhack—

PURITAN But what if Gould's need to distance himself from others was an aspect of his quest to make a coherent pattern of—[his inner life]?

PERFECTIONIST [*interrupting*] You zound like one of my patients! Introvert-extrovert! Extrovert-introvert! Flopping around like a fish on da dock! And da hypochondria—!

PURITAN You think Gould was a hypochondriac?

[THE PURITAN *begins to dress* THE PERFECTIONIST *in Gould's trademark overcoat, hat, muffler, gloves, etc.—an action that occupies them for the rest of the Variation*]

PERFECTIONIST Alienation from da body is characteristic of da schizoid personality. Hypochondria is an expression of his doubts about da validity of his own existence and fears dot others vill overvhelm and destroy him!

PURITAN Surely environmental factors have something to do with it. The man is quintessentially Canadian.

PERFECTIONIST He vas Czech!

PURITAN GOULD!

PERFECTIONIST Czech, Canuck—vats the diff? This alienation stuff transcends da geography.

PURITAN Toronto is no Prague.

[THE PURITAN *cues* THE PERFORMER]

PERFORMER [*on monitor*] That genius flourishes in isolation is a notion foreign to the Canadian psyche. Canadians huddle together for safety. The desire for security is utterly over-whelming. They ceaselessly measure and judge one another. We're not a nation of doers, we're a nation of evaluators.

[THE PERFORMER, *on the monitor, makes a sighting with binoculars held to ear. He makes notes on a clipboard*]

PERFECTIONIST Zee? Gould *hated* evaluation! He vas estranged from his country!

PURITAN Like I say, *quintessentially* Canadian.

[THE PURITAN *cues* THE PERFORMER]

PERFORMER [*on monitor, mocking* THE PERFECTIONIST] There's a relationship between northerliness and moral rectitude. The higher the latitude the greater the degree of separation from the world.

PERFECTIONIST There ve go! Glorify da prison! Fortify it with moral absolutes! Kafka said: 'One can never be alone enough when one writes—'

PURITAN '—when even night is not night enough.' I know the quote, Dr. von Krankmeister. You're missing the point. Gould honestly believed it was possible for people to show their better natures to one another without—

PERFECTIONIST [*interrupting*] Keep da verlt at arm's length! Dis is Mr. Control Freak again!

PURITAN [*cueing* THE PERFORMER] You're not *listening!*

PERFORMER [*on monitor*] Our benign neglect has left the north in something of a state of grace. Balanced against that is the spiritual depletion of a nation that has never come to grips with the mental frontiers of its own geography. I, for one, feel whole in this empty landscape. I believe that all men who encounter it singularly become, for want of a better word, philosophers.

[*Lights fade on* THE PERFORMER]

PURITAN You see, in Mr. Gould's writings—
PERFECTIONIST [*interrupting*] The octopus squirts ink to hide himself! This is nothing but damage control!
PURITAN I guess you know a thing or two about that—
PERFECTIONIST [*out of character*] What's that supposed to mean?
PURITAN What happened there? Your accent—

[THE PERFECTIONIST *pulls himself together*]

PERFECTIONIST I'm afraid this little game of yours has become rather tiresome. If you'll excuse me—

[*He starts his exit*]

PURITAN [*after him*] The truth about your friend Mr. Gould is that he lives in great psychological pain.
PERFECTIONIST [*exiting*] The truth about *your* Mr. Gould is that he is about to die.

[*The lights begin to fade. The schtick is over now.* THE PURITAN *is utterly alone in this moment*]

PURITAN [*looking at his hands*] … borrowed.

[*Lights fade. The twenty-seventh note from the ground bass sounds*]

VARIATION 27: THE HOMECOMING

THE PURITAN *studies his hands, lost in thought*

THE PRODIGY *enters, unseen and unannounced. He wears the trademark cap, overcoat, scarf and gloves. He stands where he is, watching the master in absolute awe.* THE PRODIGY *can't help himself, he kneels, cap in hand*

PRODIGY [*as* STEVEN PRICE. *New Jersey accent*] Mr. Gould?

[THE PURITAN *turns, deeply startled*]

PURITAN Who are you?

PRICE Steven Price.

[THE PURITAN *just stares*]

The front door was open. I-I had a bet on with some kids at the dorm. I said: 'I'll get down on my hands and knees in front of the guy and do two "Allahs."'

PURITAN 'Allahs'?

PRICE Sorry, about this—it's worth twenty bucks. [*prostrating himself*] Allah. Allah.

[THE PURITAN *watches all of this, bemused*]

PURITAN It's the twenty-seventh.

PRICE It's the twenty-eighth.

PURITAN It's the twenty-seventh. Or else my morning paper was delivered by a courier from Dimension X. Why are you dressed like that?

PRICE You got a bit of a following at Juilliard.

PURITAN I'm a style sample, am I?

PRICE We think you got a few moves.

PURITAN [*laughing*] That's really very funny.

PRICE I'm serious! It's not just the look. Everybody *listens* to you. There are these heated debates.

PURITAN I'll bet there are.

[THE PURITAN *starts laughing again. He can't help himself*]

PRICE —and we play the game.

PURITAN Which one?

PRICE I'm thinking of someone, guess who it is.

PURITAN [*really enjoying this*] Don't start! *Please!*

PRICE I can't believe I mixed up the stupid date.

PURITAN Performance anxiety. The hemispheres of the brain

fall out of synchronicity. Are you familiar with the work of Julian Jaynes?

PRICE *The Origins of Consciousness and the Breakdown of the Bi-cameral Mind?* Interesting book, the corpus callosum and all that, but I don't think God was an audio hallucination.

PURITAN An intriguing hypothesis, nonetheless. If consciousness itself is an expression of the Deity's intent, which I tend to believe it is, then the coded recognition of that fact would be embedded in our brain physiology and transmitted to us in a multiplicity of ways. Hearing would quite naturally be one of them.

PRICE I see what you're saying, music is sacred stuff.

PURITAN Music, fog horns, branches tapping against windows in old Trevor Howard movies, a vacuum cleaner next door—they're all part of the Deity's message.

PRICE Except music is art. The message is *about* itself.

PURITAN Is that how you know something's art? Because it's *about* itself?

PRICE That-that's one way of knowing. What do you think art is?

PURITAN A life force released *by* the noblest aspirations of man and addressed *to* the noblest aspirations of man, his conscious desire for contact with the sublime. For transcendence.

PRICE And music?

PURITAN Are you getting this down on tape or something?

PRICE It-it's a real question. I promised them I'd ask you.

PURITAN Music is a pulse of intense feeling that illuminates the means of its own transmission. A kind of pure speech for the inner ear. When I was a little boy I could sight-read from score and hear music which I had no way of playing because my hands were too small. I played it anyway, and sang the music the way I wanted to hear it when I couldn't reach the notes.

PRICE The *unheard* music!

PURITAN [*intrigued*] You've heard it?

PRICE It's what makes me believe in the world.

[*They smile, knowing instinctively that some test has been passed*]

PURITAN Well, you're here. I'm here. We might as well get on
with it. I have a few things to tell you that you may not be
ready to hear.

PRODIGY [*out of accent*] You promised you'd teach me everything you knew about playing the piano in—

PURITAN [*interrupting*] What happened there? Your accent—

PRODIGY [*out of accent*] What?

PURITAN Say 'piano.'

PRICE [*back in accent*] Piana. [*pause*] How are you going to
teach me? I'll do anything you say. Is it like an exercise?

PURITAN [*he looks at his hands*] I have nothing to teach you
about this. Playing the piano is a way of thinking. You'll see
how I think when we record together.

PRICE I'll do whatever you say.

PURITAN You'd better hear me out before you agree so readily. You
and I are going to record the Beethoven Second Concerto ...

[*Music under: Ten seconds before the piano entry in the second
Movement*]

PRICE I know. It's going to be *outrageous*. You *own* that Concerto.
You played it for your orchestral debut with Bernstein.

PURITAN And you are going to try and play the adagio section
very adagio, even slower than I played it. So slowly that the
structure almost falls apart. You're going to invite me into
the deep place between the notes.

PRICE I'll play it as slow as you want, Maestro.

PURITAN Don't call me 'Maestro.'

PRICE What do I call you then?

PURITAN You call me Glenn.

[*They look at each other for a moment.* PRICE *has to look away*]

PRICE Just tell me what to do.

PURITAN Listen to me. I know that you came here because you
   wanted to play with Glenn Gould.
PRICEY It's the dream of a lifetime.
PURITAN I'm afraid I must tell you that after we've finished
   recording I'm going to remove your performance and
   replace it with my own.
PRICE Oh.
PURITAN Everybody has their dream. You want to record with
   Glenn Gould. I want to conduct myself at the piano. We want
   different aspects of the same thing and, properly applied, tech-
   nology can satisfy both of us. I hope you're not too disappointed.
PRODIGY [*out of accent*] No. I-I'm not confused about—
PURITAN [*interrupting*] There it is again. I hear Canada in your voice.
PRICE No, sir.
PURITAN No, *Glenn*.

[THE PURITAN *looks into* PRICE*'s eyes.* PRICE *looks away*]

Have you decided on a course for your career?
PRICE I've been asked to play in Europe three months from now.
PURITAN Bravo!
PRICE I-I don't know if I'm ready.
PURITAN Move toward the unheard music. If that takes you to
   Europe, so be it.
PRICE I ... I wish I was brave like you.

[*The comment brings* THE PURITAN *up short*]

PURITAN Brave men stand in front of bullets. I'm afraid that's
   not my—
PRICE [*interrupting*] You're the bravest man I know.
PURITAN Fish swim. Birds fly. I play the piano.

[*Pause*]

PRICE Never stop. Okay?
PURITAN We'll do our best to ... to carry on.

[*Pause*]

PRICE Can I ask you a personal question?
PURITAN Depends what it is …
PRICE Are you happy?
PURITAN Sorry. Indirect questions only, please.
PRICE If I was you, what would I be?
PURITAN A man looking back at himself.

[*Pause*]

Don't be afraid in Moscow.

[*Pause*]

PRODIGY [*as himself*] You *knew*.
PURITAN Of course I knew.
PRODIGY I knew you knew.
PURITAN [*little smile*] And I knew you knew I knew. [*he hands* THE PRODIGY *a rose*] Let me see your smile …

[*The two men look into each other's eyes.* THE PRODIGY *smiles*]

PRODIGY Godspeed …
PURITAN And you too …

[*Lights fade. The twenty-eighth note from the ground bass sounds*]

VARIATIONS 28 & 29: MR. DEATH

Lights up

THE PERFECTIONIST *is buttoning* THE PERFORMER *into a white satin tuxedo shirt fitted and fastened with a hundred black dome tabs. The shirt is a cross between evening wear and a strait-jacket.* THE PERFORMER *seems at ease*

PERFORMER Not nearly tight enough. It won't do the job
unless it's snug as a bug.

PERFECTIONIST [*very cheerful*] Oh, you'd be surprised—a
strong, well-disciplined mind can prevent its own disruption
under almost any circumstances— [*tightening the bonds*] —
how's that?

PERFORMER Perfection!

PERFECTIONIST I am reminded of accounts of prisoners who
survive prolonged periods of deprivation and torture. They
stare at a wall and turn their minds into encyclopedias—
nothing but mental calisthenics from morning till night—
until every idea has been sorted, ranked, alphabetized and
cross-referenced. What I'm trying to say is there's great
freedom within total control.

PERFORMER You're telling me! I could fly like a bird! How
about a duet?

PERFECTIONIST The game? This isn't a canon.

PERFORMER Who cares? C'mon, just for old time's sake ...

PERFECTIONIST Got somebody in mind? I'm all ears.

PERFORMER I don't know. Let me see ...

[*While* THE PERFORMER *thinks he dum-dums to the unheard
music*]

PERFECTIONIST You always do that when you're trying to know.

PERFORMER I don't *try* to know, my friend, I *know*.

[*Lights up on* THE PURITAN, *sitting in the La-Z-Boy chair under
the plaid wool throw. He drowsily awakens from a dream*]

PURITAN I was receiving an honorary degree at Fordham. At
the President's dinner afterwards the chair to my right was
empty as the meal began. The place card read 'Mr. Death.'

[*Lights shift. The twenty-ninth note from the ground bass sounds*]

As soup was served I awaited this gentleman's arrival with a giddy mixture of anxiety and amusement …

PERFORMER If you were a funeral, what kind of funeral would you be?

PERFECTIONIST A cross-fade between Edith Piaf in Paris and Immanuel Kant in Konigsberg. An outpouring of emotion that is cool to the touch.

PERFORMER Large or small?

PERFECTIONIST Large and strange. A cathedral crowded to the doors. Princes kneel beside commoners. Pew upon pew of savants and sages. Then the congregation, spilling out the back of the church to stand in silence on the pavement. Bright-eyed children beside doddering old men. Rich along-side poor. They stand in the cold while the church bell tolls.

PURITAN When he finally arrived Mr. Death was a nondescript little man with round, pink cheeks and a neat moustache. He sat down beside me as the waiter was taking my soup bowl, extended a rather large hand before I'd said a word. 'Mr. Gould,' he sang, 'my apologies, rush-hour traffic, I'm John Deeth.' He pronounced it *'deeth.'*

[THE PURITAN *turns his attention to* THE PERFORMER *and* THE PERFECTIONIST, *tuning them in*]

PERFORMER A state occasion?

PERFECTIONIST No, nothing like that. More like a pause in everyone's thinking. A profound silence that seemed to issue from the landscape itself.

[THE PERFECTIONIST *and* THE PERFORMER *pause to listen to the silence.* THE PURITAN *breaks the moment*]

PURITAN And I can remember thinking: this poor little man! Forced to live, day in and day out, with the dreaded fact of that last name. 'Hello, I'm John Deeth.' And sooner or later every day he'd have to spell it for somebody and they'd say, You mean like 'death'? And he'd have to say, No, *deeth.*

[*pause*] The helpless daily horror of finding oneself caught in that act of self-deception ... and no escape from the pain of it, *ever.*

PERFORMER What would focus their grief?

PERFECTIONIST The service would be full of wonderful music.

PURITAN Human tragedy is born in a sequence of small daily falsehoods, Mr. Deeth. Take my advice, don't base your life on a mispronunciation. Be joyfully who you are. Embrace the contradictions.

[THE PURITAN *pulls the blanket around himself and dozes off again*]

Goodnight ... Mr. Death.

PERFORMER How would the body be presented?

PERFECTIONIST Unadorned. One vase of calla lilies.

PERFORMER And what would be the text for the service?

PERFECTIONIST Something from Revelation. A reading from 'Burnt Norton.' And then the final Aria from the Goldberg Variations.

PERFORMER And how will the congregation respond?

PERFECTIONIST There will be moments of incandescent grief, real as the shower of sparks from a welder's torch. The music going up and up and up. The mourners feeling that they too are part of this great unfinished journey. Canadians are a curious breed, you see. They find unity in their sense of collective loss.

PERFORMER Oh, so this is a *Canadian* funeral?

PERFECTIONIST Yes. Oh yes. Very much so. *Shh.*

[THE PERFECTIONIST *brings* THE PERFORMER *to his feet and leads him off. Lights fade. The thirtieth note from the ground bass sounds*]

VARIATION 30: THE QUODLIBET

The sequence which follows should have the feeling of the 'consciousness cascade' people who've returned from the dead ascribe to the final moments of life. A chaotic firing of cortical neurons which gradually subsides as the electromagnetic field dims and shrinks down past the brain stem. A mood of autumnal celebration

Lights up on THE PURITAN. *He's alone in front of his music stand writing on the yellow legal-length pad that rests there. He pauses*

THE PERFORMER *enters in his strait-jacket and begins a complex series of escape moves*

PURITAN I'm heading into my 'late period,' Jessie. With luck and pluck it may span the next twenty-five years. I have so many plans. I want to give up recording, stay away from the piano entirely and work on my skills as a conductor. I want to compose—I have a wonderful idea for a piece based on the Book of Revelation. But before all that I'm going to return to the concert stage for one final performance, live before an audience of dignitaries on an oil-well drilling platform in the Arctic Ocean! You think I'm kidding! I've already recorded it!

[*Music sting: The opening guitar riff from 'Sgt. Pepper's Lonely Hearts Club Band.'* THE PERFORMER *breaks loose from his strait-jacket and starts to boogie*]

PERFECTIONIST [*entering, cueing out the music*] I *need* music, not this clichéd rubbish! Chopin, Schumann and Liszt are definitely a waste of time!

[THE PERFORMER *starts to skip using the sleeves of his strait-jacket as a rope*]

PERFORMER *It's a sign of the times / That my love for you is getting so much stronger!*

PERFECTIONIST Schubert can be tolerated occasionally! All of the early Romantics can go jump in the lake except Mendelssohn.

[THE PERFECTIONIST *whirls around and begins to conduct an invisible orchestra*]

PERFORMER *When you're alone / And life is making you lonely / You can always go—Downtown.*

[*Music up: An enormous non-melodic mish-mash of strings, horns and woodwinds from various Gould recordings. A melange of melancholic styles.* THE PERFORMER *does a 'singing waiter from the Catskills' routine—a medley of Petula Clarke's greatest hits*]

PURITAN [*raising his voice over the interruption*] All kidding aside, Jessie, I have an enormous compulsion to winter over in the Canadian Arctic.

PERFORMER [*under; singing*] *I close my eyes and I can fly / And I escape from all this worldly strife / Restricted by routine of life / But still I can't discover: Who am I?*

PURITAN The mental state I must struggle to maintain living here in the south occurs as a natural human response to the pure physical reality of the far north! [*to* THE PERFECTIONIST] Keep it down!

[THE PERFECTIONIST, *lost in the oblivion of his own ecstasy, conducts even harder. The chaotic music swells another notch.* THE PERFORMER *continues his Petula Clarke medley*]

PERFECTIONIST Verdi, Puccini and the other operatic masters make me physically ill! I despise Debussy, Ravel and Poulenc!

PERFORMER [*skipping around* THE PERFECTIONIST] *My love is warmer than the warmest sunshine / Softer than a sigh / My love is deeper thant the deepest ocean / Wider than the sky.*

PERFECTIONIST [*overlapping* THE PERFORMER] Stravinsky and Bartok are the two most overrated composers of the century! Mozart, what can I tell you about Mozart? [*suddenly aware of* THE PERFORMER] Pet Clarke! Now there's a little lady who had her head screwed on!

PURITAN [*to* THE PERFECTIONIST] Control yourself!

[THE PURITAN *pulls up* THE PERFECTIONIST*'s shirt and yanks out a cord that's plugged into a socket in his chest.* THE PERFECTIONIST *freezes in mid-flail.* THE PERFORMER *passes in front of* THE PURITAN*'s music stand, tears the top sheet off the yellow pad, reads from it*]

PERFORMER [*as* THEODORE SLUTZ] —like, ah, we have a curious need to parse the unconscious, indeterminate and subliminal relationships between, ah, an artist's body of work and the society from which he comes, you know? It's like the whole historical context thing.

[THE PRODIGY *runs on-stage, interrupting* THE PERFORMER. *He runs around the stage, trailing streamers of audio tape, a kid playing a private game of make-believe*]

PRODIGY [*singing and laughing*] *I have long been away from thee!*
PERFORMER [*sings*] *I am here!*
PRODIGY [*sings*] *Beets and turnips don't suit my digestion!*
PERFORMER [*sings*] *If my mother cooked some meat—*
PRODIGY & PERFORMER [*sings*] *—I'd stay without question!*

[THE PRODIGY *tears a sheet off* THE PURITAN*'s pad and reads it breathlessly*]

PRODIGY Glenn Gould: Alter egos of. As animal lover. Artistic legacy of. Back injury of. Career of. Cars of. As celebrity.
PERFORMER [*reading over his shoulder*] Chair built for.
PRODIGY Childhood of. Concert career abandoned by.

PERFORMER Counterpoint as preoccupation of.
PURITAN [*from memory*] Creative cheating by.
PERFORMER Critics disliked by. Depression suffered by.
PRODIGY Devotion needed by. Eccentricities of ... [*continuing under*] Fan letters to. First experience of booing by. Flying feared by. Games enjoyed by. Health problems of. Honours awarded to.

[THE PURITAN *turns back to his convseration with Jessie*]

PURITAN [*overlapping* THE PRODIGY, *above*] I'd like to set up a puppy farm on Manitoulin Island—a home for all the unwanted doggies in the world. A farmhouse in a February field, grey light dissolving into grey land, and guess who is going to live there with me, Jessie? [*he smiles*] These are the happiest days of my life.
PRODIGY [*continuing under*] Hymns loved by. Insomnia suffered by. As International star. Isolation of. Lefthanded-ness of. Listener as composer in vision of. Memorization skills of. Money earned by. Newspaper written by, in childhood.
PERFORMER [*reading from* THE PURITAN*'s pad; plummy British accent*] We suffer from a perceptual bias which sees historical movements in terms of climaxes and determines the virtues of an artist according to the manner in which he participated in, or better still, anticipated, the nearest climax. [*pause, to* THE PERFECTIONIST] You, sir, are constitutionally unfit to be a rebel.

[THE PERFORMER *plugs* THE PERFECTIONIST *back in. He comes back to himself by degrees*]

Now, behave.
PERFECTIONIST [*to camera*] How was I? Like this? More like this?

[THE PERFORMER *hands him a sheet from* THE PURITAN*'s yellow pad*]

PRODIGY [*continuing under*] Perfect pitch of. Persona of. As
Prodigy ...

[THE PRODIGY *pauses, studies his hands. SFX: Arctic wind*]

PURITAN [*to Jessie*] Finally, I have an enormous compulsion to
look upon the Polar seas, Jessie. The wind has not touched
another face. It is your wind. The day is your day. The sky is
the crown of your head.

PERFECTIONIST [*reading from the yellow sheet*] I prefer the
model of Richard Strauss—a man who made much richer
his own time by not being part of it. Who spoke of all
generations by being of none.

[THE PERFECTIONIST *raises his shirt. Looks at his plug.* THE
PRODIGY *turns his attention to* THE PURITAN]

PURITAN The Goldbergs are finished now. The total ordering of
sound in time. Unity. Coherence. Structure. These are the
things that have mattered to us most. To become one with the
Absolute and become aware of that oneness—

[THE PRODIGY *smiles*]

PERFECTIONIST [*gripping his own plug*] —inside merging with
outside ... in the divine architecture of the sublime.

[THE PERFECTIONIST *hesitates in his moment of hari-kari,
summoning his resolve*]

PRODIGY As Performer ...

[THE PERFORMER *looks at* THE PERFECTIONIST]

PERFORMER I looked for a truth outside myself ... and finding
it, became part of the truth I sought ...

PRODIGY As Perfectionist ...

PERFECTIONIST Control!

[THE PERFECTIONIST *rips out his own plug and goes into a freeze*]

PRODIGY As Puritan ...

[THE PRODIGY *and* THE PERFORMER *turn their attention to* THE PURITAN. *He touches finger to forehead—the 'I know' gesture*]

PURITAN I have had a revolution in my head. I can feel ... the blood ... in my brain.

[*The other Glenns touch finger to forehead. Lights fade to black. The thirty-first note from the ground bass sounds*]

THE FINAL ARIA

Lights up. The keyboard hangs over the empty stage

Music up: Final Aria, late version

With the first note of the Aria, eight white-gloved hands come into the light from below and begin to play and conduct. All the hands share the same slow, deliberate performing energy

Mid-way through the Aria the hands begin to conduct each other. They move, sensuous as underwater sea fans or the undulating legs of a centipede. A feeling of great harmony and unity here

PRODIGY Physical space is an alluring distraction.
PERFORMER Chronological time a trap.
PERFECTIONIST We are each our own creation.
PURITAN We will a world into being ... and fill it with ...
ALL —ourselves.

In the final bars of the Aria the hands drop out of the light one by one. The final hand holds one finger aloft to sustain the decay of the last note of the Aria. This hand too disappears as the thirty-second note from the ground bass reverberates down to silence. Lights fade to black

CODA

A single church bell tolls, melancholic and forlorn. This bell is joined by another bell, a higher sonority that rings down across it. Other bells peel into the mix, carillons from the spires of the great cathedrals ringing in a celebration that lifts the mood of the moment and carries us up and up and up

The players take their bows amid this glorious tintinnabulation. Each of them throws a single rose to the crowd

Cover Design: Gordon Robertson
Cover photo: Courtesy the CBC, Sony Canada, and the Estate
of Glenn Gould. Used by permission.
Printed in Canada

COACH HOUSE PRESS
401 (rear) Huron Street
Toronto, Canada
M5S 2G5